I0721359

The Secret Statutes of The Templars

The Secret Statutes of The Order of The Templars

Dr. J. F. L. Th. Merzdorf,
of
Oldenburg, Germany

First Published 1877

First English Translation by

Tracy R. Twyman

2018

ISBN: 978-1-962312-08-0

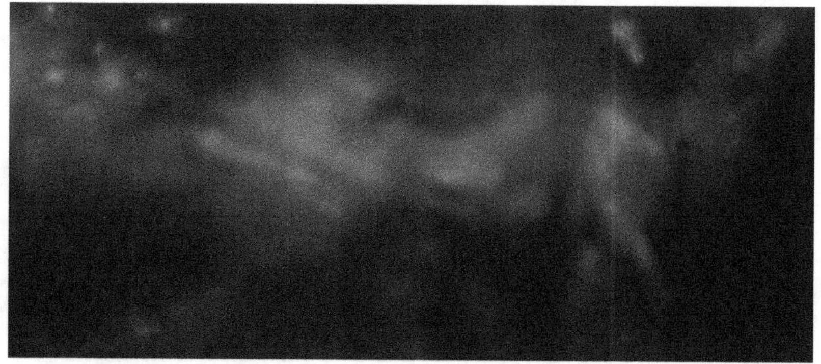

"But what do these ridiculous monsters, these horrible beauties and beautiful horrors mean in your cloisters, where the monks do their reading? half-men, these motley tigers, these soldiers who fight and these hunters who give the horn? Here we see a single head for several bodies or a single body for several heads: there it is a quadruped with a serpent's tail further on it is a fish with the head of a quadruped. Sometimes we see a monster which is a horse in front and a goat behind, or which has the head of a horned animal and the back of a horse. Finally the number of these representations is so great and the diversity so charming and so varied that one would rather look at these marbles than read in manuscripts, and spend the day admiring them than meditating on the law of God. have no shame in such frivolities, we should at least s regret what they cost."

(Excerpt from the Apology of Saint Bernard *Apologia ad Guillelmum,* 1125, addressed to Guillaume, Abbé de Saint-Thierry)

Baphomet, Sant-Sernin de Toulouse
From:
www.lesfilsdelavallee.fr

Table of Contents

Secret Statutes of the Templars Translated to English 1

Preface 3

Content 5

Introduction 6

Foreword 30

So begins the path of the poor brothers of the Temple in the holy city 33

1. How to receive the sacred service. 33

2. How much to pray Our Lord's Prayer when prevented from attending Sunday service. 33

3. What to do for deceased brothers 33

4. The chaplains should only have maintenance and clothing. 34

5. About the deceased knights, who are at their end. 34

6. No brother should offer a sacrifice. 34

7. About the immutable standing. 35

8. Concerning the feeding of the Convent. 35

9. From the lecture. 35

10. Of the enjoyment of the flesh. 36

11. How the brothers should eat. 36

12. Two or three rations of lentils will suffice on other days. 36

13. Which food to enjoy on Friday. 36

14. That Grace is to be said after eating. 36

15. The tithe of bread is to be received by the almsman. 37

16. That the meal is at Master's discretion. 37

17. After completing the Complete is silent. 37

18. That the fatigued do not need to get up for Matins. 37

19. That the communion of feeding will always be preserved among the brethren. 38

20. About the style and quality of clothing. 38

21. The servants must not wear white smocks. 38

22. Only the knights are allowed to wear white clothes. 39

23. That one uses the lambskins. 39

24. The old clothes are to be distributed among the arms carriers 39

25. Who wants the best, should receive the worse. 39

26. Consider the size and texture of the dress. 39

27. The draper observes the equality above all. 40

28. The excess of hair. 40

29. From beaks and bows. 40

30. About the number of horses and servicemen. 40

31. No one is allowed to beat a vain serviceman. 40

32. How to take on the followers. 40

33. That no one conduct himself as according his own will. 41

34. When allowed without master's order to go through the city 41

35. Whether allowed to go alone. 41

36. No one is allowed to demand what he needs on the fly.. 42

37. Concerning bridles and spurs. 42

38. Spears and shields should have no overlays. 42

39. About the power of the Master. 42

40. Concerning satchels and bags. 42

41. Of letters. 43

42. On blurting off fabulations.. 43

43. [Regarding] acquisition and acceptance. 43

44. From the food bags of the horses.................................. 43

45. That no one seeks to trade or to demand goods. 44

46. No one should catch birds with birds, nor operate with a bird catcher.. 44

47. That no one should shoot with a bow or crossbow. 44

48. That the lion is always to hunt. 44

49. In every investigation of you, ye shall hear the judgment. 45

50. That this rule is kept in all its parts. 45

51. That all knights are allowed to have goods and people. . 45

52. Care must be taken for the sick. 45

53. For the weak, the necessary is always enough. 45

54. No one shall provoke anger to others............................. 46

55. How to keep married brothers.. 46

56. The sisters may no longer live in the house of the men. . 46

57. That the temple brothers should not associate with the excommunicated. 46

58. How to take in secular knights. 46

59. Not all brothers are called to the secret assembly. 47

60. One should pray silently. 47

61. The servants shall be taken in oath. 47

62. Boys, as long as they are still unexperienced, may not be made temple-brothers... 47

63. The elderly should be honored. 48

64. Of the brothers who travel through the various provinces. 48

65. The food should be distributed evenly. 49

66. The temple brothers should have tithing. 49

67. About the heavy and light offenses. 49

68. Regarding guilt which a brother does not recognize as such. 49

69. From Easter celebrations to All Saints' Day, linen shirts may be worn. 50

70. How many and which pieces are necessary for a bed. 50

71. Loose talk is to be avoided. 50

72. All women's kisses are to be avoided. 51

New additions to the rule of the Poor Soldiers of the Holy City. 52

1. That the brothers of the Temple Order should wear a red cross on their mantle. 52

2. What banner the brothers should have. 52

3. Regarding the seal of the brothers. 52

4. About the punishments of perishing brothers. 52

5. That the brothers owe obedience to the Patriarch of Jerusalem. 53

6. That the brothers are to work. 53

7. How the brothers ought to be bought back from captivity. 53

2. Here begins the secret statutes which have given the elect to brothers of the temple order as they, the brothers Roger of Montagu, Preceptor of Normandy, and Robert of Barr, procurator of the religious houses there, received them. 54

1. Of the last times. 54

2. Of the secret chapters of the Chosen. 54

3. About the way to hold a chapter. 54

4. How the brothers are called to the secret chapter. 55

5. Like the brothers who are still attached to the church of Antichrist. 55

6.How [to speak to] chosen brothers who continue to be in turmoil. 55

7. What to teach the edited brothers afterwards. 56

8. The despisers of the common rule are not called to the stage of the elect. 56

9. Brothers inexperienced in the first elements of knowledge are not to be included. 57

10. That Arefast's descendants are not to be included among the elect. 57

11. How to take up the brothers. 57

12. What the brother to be included in the chapter has to swear. 58

13. From the confirmation of the oath. 58

14. Of the despisers of Christ. 59

15. Prohibition of the publication of the articles of association, conclusion of the chapter and various types of recording. 59

16. How many times in the year the secret statutes are revealed to the brothers. 60

17. Law and Doctrine of the Chosen. 60

18. About the synagogue of Antichrist. 61

19. At the mercy of the chosen ones. 62

20. From the faith of the chosen ones. 62

21. The freedom of the chosen. 63

22. From fasting. 63

23. On the Traffic of the Chosen with the Unbelievers. 63

24. Of the journeys of the chosen ones. 64

25. Observation of the general rule and of confession. 64

26. The right of the Chosen in the government of houses. 65

27. On the construction of workshops and other secret facilities. 65

28. Of libraries and studies. 66

29. Of the betrayal and swearing. 66

30. Of the death and burial of the elect. 67

3. Here begins book of the baptism of fire [*Consolamentum*], or the book of the secret statutes, which Master F. Roncelius has written down for the consoled brothers of the Temple Militants. 68

1. Concerning the light of baptism of fire [*Consolamentum*]. 68

2. Concerning the adherence of the consoled brothers. 68

3. Concerning the true religion. 68

4. Concerning the mystery of the consoled. 69

5. Concerning the love of the consoled to all. 69

6. Of the external conduct of the consoled. 69

7. Concerning the wisdom of the consoled. 70

8. Of those who can be admitted to the nighttime chapters of the baptized [*consolati*]. 70

9. Concerning hospitality. 71

10. How to deal with resident brothers. 72

11. As with the monks, clerics, abbots, etc. 72

12. As with the laity. 72

13. How the baptism of fire [*Consolamentum*] is performed in the chapter. 73

14. The prayer of Moses. 74

15. The prayer of the Son of Mary, called Jesus. 74

16. The prayer of Baphomet. 75

17. About the unveiling of the idol. 75

18. The completion of the baptism of fire [*Consolamentum*]. 76

19. Concerning the practice of arts. 76

20. Concerning elections.. 77

4. Here begins the registration of the secret signs, which Master F. Roncelinus has put together.. 78

Postscript.. 82

Secret Statutes of the Templars Translated to English

Thanks to Harrison Lindenfield, who graciously provided me with a rough translation of this document, then worked with me on the editing thereof, and allowed me to publish it, I am pleased to present the world's first English translation of *The Secret Statutes of the Templars*, discovered by Theodor Merzdorf in a Masonic library, having been copied from a document found in the Vatican Archives, and then translated by him into German, and published 1877, shortly after Merzdorf's sudden and early demise at age 29.

The authenticity of these statutes has been a matter of controversy for almost 150 years, but due to the language barrier, few in the English-speaking world are familiar with them. My own investigation into the matter of the Templars, detailed in my book *Baphomet: The Temple Mystery Unveiled* (co-written with Alexander Rivera), indicates that these statutes may very well be authentic, for the practices detailed therein– spitting on the cross, exposure of the "male member" during initiation, the repetition of Islamic prayers, and fraternizing with the Saracen enemy, along with Druzes, Cathars, Bogomils, and other heretics, as well as the worship of the idol Baphomet–are all consistent with the continuum of tradition that connects the Templars with their Gnostic predecessors, and their Freemasonic descendants, according to our research.

The content here is also consistent with the revelations contained in the Chinon Parchment, detailing the confessions that Templars made to Pope Clement V, which were discovered in the Vatican Archives in 2007 and released by Vatican spokeswoman Barbara Frale in 2011. Part of what connects all the seemingly disparate sects within the continuum of tradition previously mentioned is a belief that those who have received the "Baptism of Wisdom"–called here the Baptism of Fire–are literally above the law: not just man's law, but the law of Moses–so that nothing they choose to do may be counted against them.

We find this attitude in sects as far-flung as the Ismailis of the Middle Ages and modern Aleister Crowley following "Thelemites." It is, most likely, what was meant when it was said that the Cathars (a.k.a. the Albigensians) could "no longer sin" after they went through the sacred *consolamentum* rite, or the "Rite of Perfection," alleged in these documents to have been practiced by the Knights Templar as well.

Now I present to you, below, the Merzdorf document, containing "The Secret Statues of the Templars," including "The Book of the Baptism of Fire," translated into English for the very first time:

> **The secret statutes of the order of the Templars after the copy of a manuscript allegedly in the Vatican archives, published for the first time in the Latin original and in German translation, issued by Dr. Merzdorf, Grand Ducal Oldenburg senior librarian.**
>
> **A contribution to the history of the Order of the Temple and Freemasonry supplementing Wilcke's work on the Order of the Order of the Temple.**
>
> **With a postscript from Dr. Enftav Schwetschke.**
> **Halle, G. Schwetschke'scher Verlag.**
> **1877**

Preface

On the following pages the print of a manuscript is presented, the contents of which appear to be of great interest.

These are the secret statutes of the temple-masters, which one probably supposed, but which until now had eluded the public.

The exact print of the copy of the originals allegedly in the Vatican Archives in the Examination Documents of the Order of the Templars is here given and submitted to the approving or rejecting judgment, especially the church historian, since we ourselves dare not affirm or deny the authenticity of the church; both views speak of weighty reasons, the consideration of which must therefore be left to those who survey these statutes with a completely prejudicial sense and purview. In the introduction, an attempt has been made to give hints to both sides, which may well be worth the trouble of pursuing further.

Oldenburg.

Merzdorf.

Content

- Introduction
- *Monumenta ad disciplinam arcanum fratrum militia Templi descripta in archive Vaticano*
  (Monuments to the Secret Doctrine of the Brothers of the Knighthood of the Temple, Written in the Vatican Archives)
- *Regula pauperum commilitonum Christi templique Salomonis* (Rule of the poor comrades of Christ and Solomon's temple). The already known Trecensian rule.
- Prologus (Preface)
- The Trecensian Rule (Latin and German)
- New additions to the rule (Latin and German)
- *Statuta secreta* (the Secret Statutes) (Latin and German)
- *Liber consolamenti* (the book of baptism of fire) (Latin and German)
- *Rotulus signorum arcanorum* (directory of secret characters) (Latin and German)
- Postscript

Introduction

It is well known that the founders of the Temple Order made their first vows before Guaremund, the Patriarch of Jerusalem, in the name of the sweet Mother of God, to be ready for the continued service of the Savior. They accepted the rule of the regulated canons of St. Augustine, according to which they vowed chastity, obedience and poverty, adding to these three vows as the fourth: the protection of the pilgrim's road in the holy land. This latter pious purpose, which corresponded so completely to that time and its views, soon led them patrons and comrades. Bernard of Clairvaux was one of the first, and he devoted himself to the new little cooperative most zealously, and promised to obtain ecclesiastical confirmation at the forthcoming Council of Troyes. In the year 1128, under the patronage of St. Bernard, the Society was established as a religious knightly order (*militia*), and through it received a rule which is most similar to that of Benedictines and Cistercians. This rule–called the Trecensian [of Troyes]–is no longer present in its original form (the original manuscript was lost in the fall of Accon in 1291) and was first published in *Miraei deliciis ordinum equestrium* [(*origines equestrium sive militarum ordinum*), Miraeus's favorite *The Origins of the Knights and the other Military Orders*] 1613, and then reprinted repeatedly. Although the monastic side of the Order is still quite clearly recognizable in it, it is already very chivalrously colored, which is to a greater extent the case of the Statute Book, which may well have been preserved in the period from 1170 to 1230. The same was first published in an adaptation by Münter after a manuscript of the Corsican Library in Rome in 1794, and finally in the original after three different complementary manuscripts by Maillard de Chambure (*Règle et Statuts des Templiers*, Paris 1841). Here comes the knight in his right and the monk is completely gone. Yet we have not to do with these two legislations here, but rather with the secret statutes, which have completely escaped the eyes of the uninitiated.

In the trial against the Order of the Templars many statements are made, from which one can conclude a secret rite and a secret doctrine, whose well-known statutes [they] do not mention and which–as some statements prove–were not known to all

Templars. With great difficulty and care, Loiseleur, in his *doctrine secrète des Templiers*, extracted from the testimony of the Templars in Tuscany the various accusations, confirming them, and drawing attention to the connection that the Templars could have had in their secret chapters with the various heretical sects of the Middle Ages. But all this can be laboriously put together only from the various statements. An authentic compilation or even a statute book was not known, although from various statements the existence of such a compilation arises, usually with the expressions: *puncta ordinis, puncta religionis, observantia ordinis* **[if the order and the religion note it, then the order shall heed it]** is designated. Gervasius de Belvaco Michelet I. p. 175.) says: *"quod habebat quondam librum parvulum, quem bene ostendebat, de statutis ordinis; sed alium secretiorem habebat, quem pro toto mundo non ostenderet"* **["The order once kept a little document concerning their statutes, which it promoted well; but the order also had another, more secret set of statutes, which the order may not have shown to whole of the earth as likewise."]** ibid. P. 177: *"Item ex eo quia audivit pluries, quod quidam Templariorum nomine Gervasius, de quo desposuit magister Radolphus de Praellis, habebat quondam librum continentem plura statute dicti ordinis, qui videbantur ipsi testi satis bona, cui dixit: alia sunt statute in ordine nostro, quam sint ista. Et idem frater Gervasius dicebat quasi gemendo, quod errant alia puncta in dicto ordine, quae non auderet alicui revelare et, si revelaret, haberet de hoc multum pati."* **["Because it also heard many things from this, because a certain member of the Templars by the name Gervasius, whom Master Randolphus de Praellis had laid off, once used to have a document containing the many statutes spoken of the order, which itself was being seen as good enough evidence, said to him, 'There are other statutes in our order, whatever they may be.' And this same Brother Gervasius used to say this as if lamenting, because he was unable to remember the points of the oral code, which he may not have heard well enough to reveal to anyone and, if he would have revealed them, he would have struggled through the many parts."]** Gerhardus de Caus, a chief witness, who is very detailed in his statements, says (Michelet, pp. 388 ff.): *"Item dixit, quod Magister et praeceptores provinciales non sustinebant, quod aliqui fratres ordinis haberent in scriptis et penes se retinerent regulam eorum, vel statute facta post dictam regulam, nec aliqua alia continencia statute et puncta ordinis sine licencia ipsorum et videtur ipsi testi quod hoc esset male factum* *et quod ex hoc esset suspicion contra eos, et dixit se vidisse ultra mare semel vel bis quod Magister dicti ordinis, qui nunc est, precepit quod omnes fratres dicti ordinis habentes se aliquos libros tangentes regulam, statute et puncta ordinis apportarent ei, et cum fuissent apportati audivit idem testis dici, et credit quod dictus Magister faciebat aliquos comburi et aliquos reddi aliquibus ex antiquioribus ordinis, et aliquos penes se retinebat. Et idem testis dixit se tradidisse eidem testi et audivit dici a quibus dam antiquis ordinis quod fratres Guillelmus de Bellojoco et Thomas Bererdi magistri quondam ordinis consimilia fecerant et erat vox communis in ordine inter antiquos ordinis, quod ex quo literati fuerant inter eos, ordo non fecerat profectum suum."* **["Likewise he said this, because the Master and provincial leaders were not supporting him, because any other brothers of the order would keep it in writing and preserve their precept under his power, or because the statute was written down after the spoken rule, and somehow no other supporting note or statute of the order without its own independence and seen as evidence in itself which would be a bad forgery and because there would be suspicion against them, and he said that on occasion he saw it in Outremer, even twice, because the man who is now Master of the spoken order ordered all those brothers of the spoken order, who had those books mentioning the precept, the ones conveying the statutes and points of the order, to bring them forward, and once they had, he heard the same witness be stated, and he believed him because the Master having spoken this caused some books to be burnt up and some others to be given back [along with] those things from the older orders, and he retained those under his power. And the same witness, said that he bequeathed it even to this same witness and he heard it being said by a certain old order [concerning] Brothers Guillelmus de Bellojoco and Thomas Bererdi, once masters of the order, that they had once made a very similar charge and that this was a common statement among the older ranks in the order, since at that time they had been the literate among among them, the order had not made their own progress."]**

From these statements, to which we could easily add several more, we find that we were most anxious to remove these secret statutes from the eyes of the uninitiated, and especially the investigating commission. [Yet we] completely failed, because

Stephanus de Neriaco Wichel. I. p. 458) states: "*quod in alia litera erat quaedam alia in qua idem magister passagii significaverat memorato Magistro ordinis, quod illa statuta ordinis quae facta fuerant apud Castrum Peregrini, iam errant revelata.*" [**"Because in the other letter was a certain other matter in which the same master of the Pasagians pointed out to the memorialized Master of the order, that there had been statutes of the order composed near Pilgrim's fortress, which now revealed become lost."]** Nevertheless, these statutes do not appear in detail in the trials, which can only be explained by the fact that the papal commissaries convinced the reluctant Pope Clement V, who knew even before his elevation to the papal chair the offenses of the Order; but put no pressure about it on King Philip (who, even though he had internally renounced the Roman throne, was a faithful servant of papal power), that [making them known would have been] potentially destructive, and thus they chose to either completely destroy or reduce the small number of [copies of the] statutes still existing, though numerous Templars, especially their superiors, had certainly hurried to destroy all the evil sacred <infernal> writings. Individual documents were preserved with all the examination papers in the papal archives, from which the prints printed here should also be derived; as we know, for example, that Münter made excerpts from Rome of various papers, but some documents, e.g. an "*informatio super praeceptores militum templi*" [**"information above the instructors of the temple militants"]** were so affected with moisture and worms that they were completely illegible.

Let us recall that from the trial documents and testimonies we can put together the following accusations: 1) denial of Christ and mocking of the cross. 2) devil worship and sorcery, 3) adoration of an idol, 4) contempt for the sacraments and omission of the Sacramental words in the Mass, 5) heresies in confession, 6) scandalous kisses, 7) girding with the belt and 8) evil call of the Order; and if one compares these accusations with the present statutes, one will not be able to ignore the view that these statutes coincide perfectly with those statements, and that therefore one may well be inclined to believe them to be outright. The Templars had met with all sorts of opinions and views in their dealings in various countries, and in the Thirteenth Century were no longer primarily the fighters for the Holy Sepulcher, but were men who gained political influence and became a state within a state which they were well able to establish by virtue of their great privileges, their wealth, their prestige, their numerous connections, and family relationships, all the more so as they, because of the efforts of princely forces, became loyal servants and friends of the Roman throne in the struggle with the same representive worldly powers. This external political advantage outweighed the internal division of the Roman See itself, the first reason of which is to be sought in the 1162 edition of the Order's Bull; which, since none of the clergymen joining the Order of the Temple demanded and took higher steps in the Roman hierarchy, gradually loosened the bond with Rome so that only the connection between Pope and Master of the Order remained. Incidentally, the teachings and deviations of the temple masters were as completely unknown to the Romans as were those of the other religious orders of knighthood, as was the case with the letter of Pope Gregory IX to the Master of the Knights Hospitalier in 1238 – at the time when the heresies began to spread very much – it is clear: "*caeterum plures ex fratribus vestris de haeresi probabili haberi dicuntur ratione suspecti*" and Pope Innocens III. (Epp. Innoc. III ed. Balaze II. 68 ep.121) writes in 1208 to the master of the Templars: "*Ecclesiae generalis et cupiditatis anhelantes non declinant mendacia, dum utentes doctrinis daemoniorum… post haec et alia nefanda apostolicis privilegiis, quibus tam enormiter abutuntur, essent merito spoliandi etc.*" **["Falsehood does not stray away from those panting of passion nor even from the generals of the Church, while enjoying the doctrine of demons... before these and other wickedness to apostolic privileges, to which so egregiously squandered, would merit defrocking."]** Even Pope Clement IV warned [them] in 1265 before an investigation, which could not and would not turn out well. But the matter of which he had no better knowledge, and which, for the reasons indicated above, could not be obtained, and perhaps [he] did not want to have, was based on himself until he was compelled by the royal power to obtain the order entirely through the bull: *ad providam Christi vicarii* in which it is said that the unfortunate, heretical and immoral mistakes of the Christendom are kept in a concealed record for the sake of the unwashed and the profane. Here is another reason why the trial documents (even this bull) and everything related to them were unknown for a long time. How much more must this have been the case with these heretical secret statutes, which fully subscribed to the teachings of the Cathars and other sects.

The dissemination of such heretical views emanated from the Orient, where especially in Syria, Armenia, and Asia Minor the most varied Christian sects had their playground and were not quite free from Mohammedan views. We also know that the temple masters were said to have had closer contact with the Assassins, which is unproven, of course, while it is certain that their contact with the Saracens took place many times (see Michelet's IS 187) and in the friendliest terms, eg, 1244; which is not surprising, if one remembers that King Frederick II, who had versed himself completely in the Muhammadan language in Italy and best represented the type of that time in terms of his religious views, supposedly broadcast the statement that the world was betrayed by three deceivers, namely, Moses, Christ, Mohamed. From the Bulgarians, to the old heretic seat, to the Hebrews, from the southern tip of Italy to northern France, and beyond, the Antichristian directions were spread among all sorts of forms and sects, which exerted influence on all sides, to which the Knights Templar could not escape. They had their roots in the East, as can be seen from Michelet I, p. 237, and Loiseleur, p. 173, which our present authors confirm by saying in Paragr. VII. That the Statutes of *Electi* speak of the visionaries: "*qui ex transmarinis regionibus venerunt, quos coelesti cibo pastos et interna societate, recreates praesumimus videre persaepe visiones angelicas etc,*" **["Those who came from the regions of Outremer, which are fed with heavenly food and inward communion, we anticipate the restored to see angelic visions very often etc,"]** and in Par. XVII "*quam (legem) a patribus et magistris nostris trans mare accepimus etc.*" **["We received the law from the fathers and our masters in Outremer."]**

If one asks about the time when these heretical views and ceremonies were performed by the Templars, then the hints of the trials point to the years 1250 – 1270 as the time of introduction. The time of the last four grandmasters is often cited as the one in which the peculiar cult was introduced, and become the grand masters Thomas Berard and Wilhelm Beaujeu, the English provincial masters Adelard (after 1250), Himbert Peraut, William de la More, a nameless provincial master of Burgundy (Michelet II, p. 224), who is probably the same person mentioned with Procelinus or Roncelinus in Dupuis, pp. 18, 212, 314, who is also the master of Aquitaine and Poiteau Godfrey de Gonavilla (Michel II, p. 398), says that the use of the denial of the cross results from him: "*hoc facias audacter, ego iuro tibi in periculo animae meae quod numquam preiudicabit tibi quantum ad animam et conscienciam: quia modus est ordinis nostri, qui erat in carcere cuiusdam Soldani, et non poterat evadere, nisi iuraret quod si evaderet, ipse introduceret istum modum in ordine nostro, quod omnes qui reciperentur recedet o abnegarent Jesum Christum et ita fuit observatum semper.* [**"You may boldly make-what-you-will of this, I swear to you at risk of my soul, which will never mislead to you as to the extent of soul and conscience: because it is the method of our order, which was in the prison of a certain Soldanus, and he was not able to avoid it, he should not be swearing oaths even if he were avoiding it, he would introduce that method into our order himself, because all those who would be received, he will shrink oh they will deny Jesus Christ and thus he will always be watched."]** What that master meant is not apparent. In the testimony of Guido Delphini (Michel, I, p. 418), the name Roncelinus appears in connection with Beaujeu in the case of Accon: "*Requisitus, quos viderat recipi, dixit quod ultra mare in Acon, in loco in quo tenebatur capitulum eorum, vidit quadam die Dominica, sunt ut existimat viginti sex anni vel circa, recipi in fratrem ordinis fratrem Roncelium militem, de provincia Provinciae, per fratrem Guillelmum de Bello loco, tunc magnum Magistrum ordinis etc.*" **["The subject of concern, saw them recovered, in Accon in Outremer, in the place where their chapter was held on a certain Sunday, twenty-six years ago or thereabouts as he judges. They were recovered by a brother of the order, Brother Roncelius, a soldier, from the province of Province, and taken to the place of Brother Guillelmus de Bello, at that time the greatest Master of the order etc."]**

In the secret statutes we find this name as that of the composition of the division of the Consolamentum and of the Rotulus Signorum, which both divisions wish to be copied by Robert de Samford in 1240, who in 1235 mastered the province of England and procurator domor. King Henry III. 800 livr. Tourn. lent and called in 1244 as temple master to London.

The others besides the two men mentioned under the statutes cannot be proved, but are not improbable, since the names, probably of the same families, are found, and the Order, as is well known, especially in France, hails from aristocratic families resident there, and among his own constituents is represented mainly as a French knight cooperative. The listed names are now the following: 1) Among the additions to the Trecensian Rule Mathaeus de Tremelay 1205. A Bernhard de Tr. 1151-1153 was Grand Master of the Order and in the case files appears a priest Reinhard de Tremblay. 2) The statutes of the *Electi* are said to have gathered Roger de Montagu and Robert de Barris and written in 1252 Bernhard de St. Omer. From the family of Montagu we know the Grand Master Peter (1219-1229), and from the trials, a knight Stephan and a priest Johann; from the lineage of Bar (that will probably be Barris or Barro) the Grand Master Eberhard 1148-1149, as well as a Ritter Johann from the trials. 3) The name de St. Audomaro did not appear to us in this form, but we have found a clergyman Hellas Audemari, as well as knights Bernhard, Guigo, Johannes Ademari, which probably belong to the same family.

Let us now look at the content of the manuscript: it breaks down into four major sections, the first of which we can skip over, since it contains the well-known Trecensian Rule, with additions not found in Münter's translation and Maillard de Chambure's Originals, but which are otherwise available, as evidenced by the evidence and extracts from the services concerned.

The second section contains *statuta secreta fratrum electorum* and breaks down into thirty paragraphs, the special content of which we have also tried to substantiate by authenticating them as authentic and authoritative. The first paragraph speaks of the time which calls for repentance and proclaims the kingdom of God to those who have received the baptism of fire. The second to fourth paragraphs discuss the secret chapters and how to keep them. Paragraphs 5, 6, 7 specify how to assure [that only] suitable persons [are initiated], and how to make them suitable for admission, much like how Avonetus in Martene Thessaur. V. p. 1782 ff., tells the same thing about the Waldensians. Paragraph. 8 states that it is forbidden to transgress the general (ie Trecensian) rules of the level of the *Electi;* also, according to Paragraph 9, no one may be taken in if they have not graduated the Trivium or Quadrivium except the Saracens, since they are not touched by the New Babylonians of Rome. The descendants of Arefast, a retainer of Count Richard of Normandy, who had been the traitor of the martyrs Stephamis and Lisoi, are completely excluded from the paragraph. In the 11th and 12th paragraphs, we read of the ritual of reception (with the indecent kiss) and the deposition of the creed, which, according to paragraph 13, is hardened by desecration of the cross, whereupon the cladding took place. Paragraph 14 teaches us, however, that the scoffers and liars of Christ must be excluded, for the denial of the cross is not Christ, but the piece of wood. Paragraph 15 forbids the publication of the secret statutes, then gives instruction on how to close a chapter [Templar meeting], and describes still more special ways of making images, while paragraph 16 states that the four quarterly meetings should not be dedicated to recordings but only to administrative matters. The law and doctrine are discussed in the 17th paragraph and in the 18th, the teachings of the Roman church and their institutions are explained, while paragraphs 19, 20, 21 act on the grace, faith and freedom of the *Electi,* which can be summed up in the few words: *"omnium unus et dominus, una fides, unum baptisma, spiritus unus, pater et deus omnium, qui est super omnes et per omnes et in omnibus."* **["Wholly one and Lord, one faith, one baptism, one spirit, wholly Father and God, who is above all and through all and in all."]** The prescribed fasting is declared useless in paragraph 22, and the intercourse with the so-called infidels, the Jews, and the Saracens is permitted in the 23rd paragraph, and paragraph 24 prescribes the conduct of travel. The observation of the Trecensian Rule, as well as the confession to be given to the *Electi* alone, is enunciated in paragraph 25, and paragraph 26 decrees that, in filling the Order's offices, the *Electi* should seek to obtain these posts, with the exception of the Master of the Order, also according to paragraph 27 care should be taken for the construction of sacred rooms, for which they are ordered to use such masons whose attitudes agree with theirs. Concern for libraries and studies is dealt with in paragraph 28, while paragraph 29 gives rules on conduct before courts and in investigations that are fairly Jesuit but also found among the flagellants. The final paragraph deals with death and burial.

The third section is devoted to the degree of the *Consolati,* and comprises twenty paragraphs, the first of which speaks of the light and splendor of the *Consolamentum,* and the second of the *Consolati's* attention to the accepted doctrine of true religion, which is set out in the third paragraph of the proposition [that] God is to be worshiped in spirit and in truth. This mystery: God is love, and what remains in love abides in God, and God in it (paragraph 4), through the simple bricklayer, has become our ancestors, therefore the *Consolati* (paragraph 5), which is at the bottom ancient wisdom are built, prove love to all people, for God is powerful in all the people who call him fervently. In intercourse with others (paragraph 6), the *Consolati* should behave in such a way that they appear as Jews to Jews, as Saracen to Saracens, to the followers of New Babylon as alike, and avoid anything which could lead to inconvenience. Paragraph 7 declares that, although everything is permitted to the *Consolatis,* everything that is permitted is not necessary. They shall avoid outward appearances and therefore have in every temple-house a chamber with secret exits, so that the men of all estates, orderly, partisans, who had joined them could go out and enter without exciting suspicion and attention. Paragraph 8 discusses those who may be admitted to the nocturnal chapters of the *Consolati,* and emphasizes the importance of communicating with the saints scattered throughout all peoples and countries. They belong to the *Consolatis* in the spirit, even if they did not receive the baptism of fire. In this respect it is best to look at the brotherhood of builders, the *Boni Homines,* the poor of Lyons, the Albigensians, the Bagnolenses, the Bogomils, all of whom are worthy of the light of the *Consolimentum.* For this reason, Paragraph 9 is also prescribed for the exercise of hospitality against all, and allowed to do their religious exercises in the temple-house, and even to take up Druzes and Saracens, if not in the open chapter, but in the presence of three brothers in a sheltered place. Paragraphs 10 – 12 deal with the receptivity of the Templars, who did not come before the 35th. Initiates may be introduced over years; those of the clergy, against whom the greatest preface is to be used, they that must not therefore be taken up into the chapter itself, but secretly in the presence of three members, and the secret statutes and the whole doctrine may be disclosed to them only after a long time and after much trial. You can move faster with the laity, but before you turn them into *Electis* or *Consolatis* you must deliver them as clients to the Order.

In paragraphs 13-17 the ceremony of the *Consolamentum* performed in the chapter is described. Namely, after the initiate has made a complete written confession, he is introduced under Antiphonien, Responsorien and Pfalmgesängen in the chapter and placed in the middle of the assembled. After the song is over, all those present place their hands on their heads while praising secrecy, faithfulness, and obedience. Then he is acquitted of observing various observances of the Roman Church, whereupon the reading of the prayers of the three prophets takes place, which are listened to by all those present under various blessed ceremonies. After the prayers of Moses (Num. XIV. 17-21), the initiate has his beard and the nail of the right index finger cut, with appropriate words, followed by the prayer of Jesus (John XVII.), after which the Receptor says: This is my son to whom I am well pleased: and puts the ring on his finger as a sign and pledge of eternal union with God.

This is followed by the Baphomet prayer, which is Mohamed's, which is quite deistic and begins with the introductory words of the Koran. Then the eyelids are anointed to the newcomers, so that the light of the *Consolamentum* can be absorbed in full clarity. Now follows the revelation of the idol that is taken out of its container and shown to all present with the words, "Three are those who testify to the world, and these three are one," to which all present answer with "Yah-Allah," i.e. "the Glory of God." The idol is then kissed by all, and finally by the newcomer, who receives the laying of hands on his head, along with the words: "Now the Son of man is glorified, and God is glorified in him. Here, brothers, is a new friend of God who will talk to him whenever he wants": and then the chapter will be closed. Paragraph 18 defines another secret instruction about God, the Goddess of God, the true Christ, the true Baphomet, New Babylon, the nature of things, eternal life, the secret art, Abrac and talismans, and so on. These same things, as well as the secret signs, should remain secret to exempt clerics as long as possible. In the 19th paragraph, it is recommended to pay homage to the secret sciences such as alchemy and only with the utmost caution, doing so strictly in such houses whose members are all *Electi* or *Consolati*. Paragraph 20 sharpens the precept already given to the *Electis* to allow the offices of the Order, with the exception of the Master, to be transferred.

We can be shorter on the fourth part, consisting of 18 paragraphs, the *rotulus signorum*, since it lists only externalities–that is, signs that are needed when one believes oneself to be observed, or if one wishes to ascertain whether any one person already belongs to a narrower circle, or is worthy or unworthy of it. These are signs for Templars, clerics, masons, laymen, women (whom the Waldensians received), Saracens, *Electi*, *Consolati*; invitation to the chapter; signs of distress, clothing, secret statutes, receptivity, and so on. Such signs were known to be used by all closed guilds in the Middle Ages, in order to recognize those who did not belong to them, to exclude them, and thus to protect themselves against treachery.*

*As for such signs, there is something in the Constitutions of Clugny. B. II. E. 18., "d*e signis loquendi*" (Achery spicile. (1671) IV. P, 119) in the Constitution of the Abbot Wilhelm von Hirschau in the 17th Cap. (Hergot vetus discipl., Monastic, Paris, 1726, pp. 386 ff., Dungeon Wilhelm d. Seelige, pp. 266 ff.), as well as Martine de antiq. ritib. Eccles. Venet. 1783. 1. III. p. 290, f.

As far as the two divisions of *electi* and *consolati* are concerned, this division agrees with that of the Cathars and the Gallic Waldensians, who also had different degrees or *ordines*, namely *credentes* and *consolati*, also *perfecti* and *vestiti*. These degrees are not fully elucidated in the case of these files, but Michelet II, p. 87 is to be considered: "*dixerunt tamen quod postquam fratres steterant decem annis in ordine, explicabantur eiis plura ex punctis ordinis, quam prius, et ipse bene sciret si tamen in ordine viverat.*" [**"They however said that after the brothers had remained ten years in the order, they were shown more things from the points of the order than previously shown, and nevertheless he himself would know well if someone had resided in the order."**]

From this it is remarkable that only slowly and to the most experienced did they make these communications of the most liberal religious beliefs. Quite naturally, only the one who gave himself completely to the order, and was easily chosen to hold office and dignity, could be privy to the deepest secrets most dangerous to the order. This explains the partly contradictory and incomplete statements in the trials, and even [how it is] that Molay attained grandmasterly dignity, can be explained by the prohibition of the secret statutes, according to which no *Electus* or *Consolatus* could ever be elected Grand Master. Molay seems to have overruled this ban. The Grand Master was to form only the outward points, which was completely dependent on the members of the consecrated circle, forming a tight closed circle. And they did not want the domineering Molay, who was anxious to appear as [a] prince among the other princes.

Strange as it may seem, care should be taken in the statutes according to the content, and it is so peculiar that knowledge [of them] is only now coming to light. The trial records confirm that the content and history do not contradict. It should not be forgotten either that the Order, which sought to establish itself in France, targeted the southern part of this country, especially in Provence, at the time when the numerous Cathars held out against the King and Pope. Even the signers, compilers and transcribers of the statutes are not unknown in their main characters.

And yet the question can rightly be raised, how did it come about that these statutes made themselves completely invisible? It has already been stated that Rome's interest lay in the fact that the teachings of the Templars of the Christian community, in order not to give offense, do not portray in all their nakedness and conceal whatever possible. Later, when voices were raised against the Roman Curia, accusing [it] of violence against the Order of the Knights Templars, they were satisfied with short refusals and probably did not fully know [about] the official Roman annalists Rinaldi and Bzovius, Baronius' successor, even the test cases. When these men wrote, the Roman See had a different interest in the Protestants than in bringing the half-forgotten Templars to light. And how many treasures are still inexhaustible in the Vatican Archive; how many a piece of music may have been lost or taken to the wrong place during the processions from Menne to Rome and elsewhere! If it could be proved completely that Münter obtained the copy in Rome, and below, then there is no reason to doubt the authenticity.

Even if the statutes are based on a fiction, it is nevertheless primarily for the same purpose. For your own pleasure, no one has ever gone through this effort of determining authenticity. But those who committed fiction must have known the trial well, and one might conclude that the statutes had been put together by Philip's accomplices to exert pressure on the Pope's investigative magistrates. That way they were eight in a sense. Possible, but very unlikely. And yet, by the end of the last century, the trial works were completely unknown, just as [we remain] completely deprived of full knowledge of large unpublished portions.

So here is not the fiction to look for. But what about the traditions of the Masons? They should have been in contact with the Templars! The last century was full of this idea! And in addition, there are four passages in the present statutes, which refer to the brotherhood of builders, thus seeming to confirm the tradition of [a] connection between the Templars and the brotherhood of builders, or even the descent of the latter from the former. But these very four passages can throw the light on the Masons and whether or not they had a hand in the play [in creating these documents], [perhaps trying to] create an artificial proof of an untenable tradition. It is precisely these four passages that speak against the Masons, or at least against the claim of a connection between the Masons and the Templars, which we shall seek to prove afterwards. And the branch of the Masonic Confederation, which fights that tradition for historical reasons and declares it to be fable, has no interest in such a fiction.

The four items are: Stat. Elect. XXVII., Where the construction of the building dedicated to worship is mentioned: "*laboret ut fabrica domus, sicut consuetudines nostrae arcanae postulant, quanto citius instruatur, ad quod si haberi possit ope et arte talis magistri massonerii sibi serviet, qualem partum nostrorum filium esse cognoverit, et si is peregrinus adhuc esset, dummodo habilis sit, lumen electionis ei revelare ipsi liceat;*" **["He worked as a builder at home, just as the traditions of our mysteries claim, how readily it is taught, if accordingly it can be**

had by might or skill, he, so great of a master of masonry, serves himself, he will recognize what sort of son of ours is born, and if he is still a pilgrim, provided he is fit, the illumination of choosing may permit for him to reveal himself."] then Consol. IV., where the mystery is spoken: "*Loquimur ergo vobis Dei sapientiam in mysterio, quae abscondita est filiis novae Babylonis, quamque praedestinavit Deus per humiles operarios in lapide et caemento, ut revelarent eum patribus nostris, qui tradiderunt eam nobis filiis suis, in gloriam et salutem.*" **["We speak therefore wisdom to your God in a secret rite which has been hidden from the sons of New Babylon, God predestined each through lowly laborers in brick and mortar, so as to reveal him to our fathers, who bequeathed him to our own sons, in glory and prosperity."]** A third place is in Consol. par. VIII., where it is said of those, for whom treatment is admissible: "*Sicuti ergo magnas aedificiorum structuras fieri videtis, Magistris massoneriis ad opus confoederatis appropinquate, interrogantes eos per signa arcana et multos illorum scientiam Dei et artem magnam nosse comperietis.*" **["Therefore just as you see that the great construction of buildings takes place, so shall you approach the work with the united masters of masonry, [and] you will verify that they are familiar with the knowledge of God and the greatest arts, questioned through secret signs.]** The fourth place is in the Rotulus signorum and takes the second place (the first ones have the Templars): "*Quodsi aliquis Magister Massonerius non vulgaris homo vobis videbitur, interrogate eum: unde fabricae tuae lux oritur et si respondebit: ex Abrac, filius partum nostrorum et frater noster est.*" **["But if any one non-commoner Masonic Master will appear before you, you shall question him: from where the light of your craft originates and whether he will answer: from Abrac, he is the son born of our men and is our brother."]**

These passages not only recognize a connection between the Templar secret doctrine and the building cooperatives*, but make the latter even bearers of it and the well from which they flowed, and remind Consol. V. who are Consolati: "*cives sanctorum et domestici Dei, supraaedificati super fundamentum sapientum et sactorum antique saeculi.*" **["Citizens of the sacred and the household of God, having built wisdom over the foundation and the ancient ages of saints.]** That would be an indication of the Gnostics, especially those descended from Bardaisanites and others in Asia Minor. Is that true? Tradition? Fake? We do not know, can prove neither one nor the other, and therefore we only want to look at the alleged connection between the Templars and the Masons, which at least shows us that they are innocent of the falsification.

**The cathedral building, which was honored in 1176 by William the Good at Palelmo, shows the avoidance of the Byzantine, Latin, and Arab style, so that one can well suspect that in the building [built by the] brotherhood there, nothing other than Christian elements had preceded it. Should there be room for this presumption, then it would also be explained how the architectural symbolism (and perhaps also a deeper gnosis of the same) is interspersed with non-Christian views. Thus, the above-mentioned passages would in a sense be recognized as illegal.*

The abolition of the Knights Templar, which at the time might have counted about 20,000 members, naturally did not lack remnants that were not difficult to hide. But these possible refugees are of no importance, on the one hand, for the procreation of the Order itself, and for the salvation of the true or ostensible orders, since the conquerors were partly put to death and partly handed over to the watchfulness of the spiritual provincial dynodes. All the others tried to accommodate themselves as much as possible, which is also the case with Muratori scriptor. IX., 1017, where it says: "*Si qui ex Templariorum coetu manumissi aut per fugam abstracti condere potuerunt, projecto religionis suae habitu, ministeriis plebeiis ignoti aut artibus illiberalibus se dederant.*" **["If those who, set free or removed by flight, have been able to establish from a meeting of Templars, throwing down the trappings of their own religion, they had given themselves to plebeian service or ignoble arts."]** If we speak of Templar successors, we can divide them into two great divisions, namely, actual successors, which are 1) those Templars who joined the Hospitaliers, 2) the remnants of the Templars of King James II of Aragon in 1317, which formed in Spain and Portugal and certainly composed the standing army against the Moors, and the donated order of Montesa, which, however, entered soon and united with the 1163 donated order of Calatrava, which had received the whole Templar trove in Spain, whose purpose from the beginning was the fight with the unbelievers. 3) The Order of Jesus Christ, founded in

Portugal in 1318, whose tribe composed former Templars and who even kept the Templar clothes; in the fifteenth century it relinquished its knightly state and is now only a decorative order. All these orders are strictly ecclesiastical and know nothing of heresies.

The ambiguous, suspicious followers of the Knights Templar, based principally on the secrets of the Templar clerics, ostensibly preserved by the descendants of the Essenes, to whom the Order has ascribed an overrated reputation, are purported to have fallen into various divisions and have for the past century been in the Masonic fraternity while being scattered and driven underground. Consider the individual cases:

1) The successors of Peter Aumont. The legend of the latter, which in the last century belonged to various Masonic systems, such as Clermont, the Strict Observance, and others, runs as follows: The Grand Comrade Harris (a name as unfamiliar to the real story as the Aumont to be named), joined Masonry upon his pursuit into Scotland, to protect his life by hiding in the concealed order. Sometime later, the order's marshal Aumont, with seven knights, was also said to have done the same. After the unfortunate end of the Order and after they had learned of Molay's execution for his role in the Temple Order, they donated [themselves] to the Masonic fraternity in 1314. The head of the temple, cleric Peter of Boulogne, also fled to them. This view of ancestry was completely rejected at the Wilhelmsbad Convent in 1782, for the question: "What evidence can one teach to justify the propagation from the Order of the Temple?" was examined in 14 sessions and the sentence was stated: "We are not true and outright successors of the Templars."

2) The followers of the famous Gugomos. After this, "the holy order," [a mystic absurdity] had withdrawn in the temple orders at the time of Molay [who had also been Grand Master of this Order], and after his death the Grandmasterhood passed onto the bishops of Cyprus de Bononia, Reinald de Pruino, and Adam de Turri, who were rescued and resumed, but Aumont is said to have hid the Order under Masonry, which was later disfigured by excesses, and judicial investigations have shown that Gugomos, the earl of gullible princes,

had taken over. He was a phony of the first kind and had made his own religious order, and, by the way, was a puppet for Rosicrucian plans.

3) Similar to these sequels are those [told of] by the infamous Starck, [who] considered the Chivalric Order of the Templars unimportant, but instead declared that the clerical order had survived in Scotland and entered Freemasonry. This view was grafted onto the Strict Observance and was based on the flight of Peter of Boulogne and on the unproven assumption that the clerics had played a major role in the Temple Order. This clerical order, whose complete Latin works from Starck's hand have been before us, soon disappears again, and we can assure you that in these documents, which are very clever, none of our Templar secret statutes can be found, and instead they are completely Catholic liturgies.

4) The Swedish Masonic system with its followers in Berlin and Copenhagen. Here's another sequel legend. An otherwise unknown Knight Beaujeu, a purported nephew of Grand Duke William of Beaujeu, who fell in 1291 at Accou, is initiated by Molay in prison into the secrets of the Order, which he brought to Scotland with his helpers after Molay's death, where it became the clerical branch of the Order, while Harris and his successors continue the Order to the present day under the cover of the Masons. The secrets consist in a kind of theosophy that permeates the philosophy of all peoples, but culminates in Christ. But neither in the so-called Ekleff's Works, which form the basis, nor in the later additions, is there any trace of our *Secret Statutes*.

These four divisions form together a great class whose legends more or less approach each other and resemble each other in their original sense.

5) The successors of Larmenius or the (Parisian) new templars, a child of this century. Their motto is as follows: Molay has designated as his successor Johannes Marcus Larmenius Hierosolymitanus, who secretly collected the scattered brothers after Molay's death and propagated the secret doctrine, which was contained in two writings,

The Leviticon and *The Evangelicon*. The order of these Templars is laid down in a *Transmission Charter*. But it is a pity that this deed was fabricated by a learned antiquarian, the Jesuit Bonanni. These new templars have absolutely nothing to do with the Masonic covenant.

6) The Scottish Templars, who fall into the following subdivisions:

a) Those who joined Robert Bruce as refugees and fought for him in the battle of Bannockburn in 1314, for whom, according to the legend, the foundation of the secular Order of the Thistle of St. Andrew took place, from which later the Masonic St. Andrew degree and the Heredom of Kilwinning ritual is said to have emerged.

b) Those who joined the Knights of St. John and laid the foundation for a Masonic degree of the Knights of Malta, which proliferates especially in North America.

c) The Fraction, which claims that since Molay it has preserved its purity and is unrelated to the Masonic covenant.

7) The English Templars namely:

a) The Knights of Baldwin, dating back to the time of Richard the Lionheart.

b) The Great Commandery of England, which is the only legitimate supreme authority of the Order in England and Wales, but without proof.

8) The Templars of Ireland and America, who trace their origins back to nos. 6 and 7.

Only 1 - 4 of these eight rubrics are considered, but the tables of continuation by the Masons are much the same, so there is no mention of the past connection of the Templars with the huts, which [is something that] seems so suspicious to us in the *Secret Statutes*. There are all sorts of Masonic fictions on the other side, but in this direction we can assure you [that we] never found the slightest trace. It should also not be forgotten that those Masonic groups which, like the existing Swedish rite, assume a connection with the Templars, even if they are not strictly ecclesiastical, call themselves Christian, that is to say, Jews and Saracens, which the Statutes call their own ranks to be separate from. Such a demand completely contradicts their views. After this side, we are convinced that the creator of the fiction is not to be found.

And then another question arises: who would be the forger? He would have to be well-acquainted with the heretics of the twelfth and thirteenth centuries, and should have been able to have a greater insight into the complete investigation. The latter seems almost impossible though, because Dupuy first published in the 17th century, which was a work looted many times later in the religious history of the Masons. Some of the documents were made known, for the Dane Moldenhawer did not submit them to the public until 1792, but the original text was published in full in Michelet 1840-51. And the copy which we had has been demonstrably quiet in Petersburg since the beginning of this century!

According to our personal knowledge of the men who might have had a special interest in welding together the Masonic Confederation with the Templars, there are only three who can therefore be suspected of having no one among the known members of Clermont's system and Strict Observance who could have boasted such a knowledge, von Hund also with foundation of the Strict Observance was without any historical papers and those later, gradually, were admirably served by Starck. The author is not to be found in Sweden either, since this tradition does not exist there, and Eckleff is too insignificant to do the same, and any other forgeries are due to a certain Plumenöck (?) and Starck.

Those three men are Karl Eberhard Wächter (later v. W.) born May 21, 1746, died May 25, 1825(?); Gottlieb Freiherr von Gugomos, whose year of birth and death [are] unknown; Joh. Aug. Starck (later by St.) born October 28, 1741, died March 13, 1816. Of them, however, the first two, clever and cunning as they might be, were too ignorant to build these statutes themselves. There was also Watchman, who was probably a Jesuit-Rosicrucian Emissary, with the last Stuart in

Jutland, in order to pass on his alleged hereditary Grand Mastership of the Masons to another princely head (who succeeded Gustav III, King of Sweden, in 1783, but only against a fair bit of money), also lay guard, say, less in the connection with the condemned temple-masters than in the acquisition of property, in which he sought the true secrets of the high order. He seems to have succeeded in this, for he, who had gone to Italy poor, returned rich, and his theological teachings–incantations of Theosophy–often attracted to him personages great and small, including the Duke Ferdinand of Brunswick, Landgrave Carl von Hessen- Cassel, Duke Carl of Südermanland (later king Carl XIII of Sweden), and the crown prince (later king) Frederick William II of Prussia, who he brought into his net and who filled his pockets with real treasures, while he imagined ideals. The knowledge necessary [to perceive] falsification fell away from him, [even] more so [towards] the notorious Abentheurer Gugomos, although he knew how to convince gullible princes, especially those of Hesse-Darmstadt, Mecklenburg, and Nassau. But his glory did not last long, and he himself had to write a judicial revocation in 1780, in which he confesses that his teachers (Jesuits and especially Rosicrucians), who wanted to break the Masonic covenant, had been his teachers and deceivers.

A very different personality is the third, Starck, who died as an evangelical court preacher to Darmstadt under the not entirely unfounded suspicion of [being] a crypto-Catholic. He was a very learned, but also very addicted, man, who went to Petersburg before he went to Mitau. For years he had stopped in Paris and rummaged through archives and libraries, where it might have been possible to give him an insight into the testimony of the Templars kept at St. Germain des Pres near Paris. Later, in Germany, he sought to find an entrance to a special Masonic species, which he called the clerical (although he had no idea of it alone), but was shipwrecked. After this failure, he raised his predecessors and rivals from the saddle of the abovementioned princes (especially those of Darmstadt and Mecklenburg, whom he had previously known to win and approach), and inherited their inheritance by forming a secret society, "the seven allies," driven mainly by Theosophy (and at the same time as [the popularity of] alchemy [among clerics]), it would be presumed that this association, which was so incidentally concerned with the religious views of all times, would have been endowed with these statutes by Starck, but this is contradicted by a passage in his *Apology of the Order of the Freymourists*–and Masons had to be the allies–in which he expresses the capacity of absorption as follows: "We choose the one who is most in tune with the nature of the deity, we allow all Christians (for Jews, Gentiles and Turks can never claim our secrets, even if we are reproached for allowing some unimportant Masons to admit Jews) our order, we love them with brotherly love, without having to be led by a blind zeal to worry about [the particular opinion of] each one." Add to this Starck's other views, and especially the whole up-to-now unprinted (but seen by us) correspondence of "Seven allies," in which just the slightest hint of these statutes can be found. Although Starck may not be far from all kinds of fiction and subductions of strange documents, he is innocent of [concocting] these statutes.

Certainly none of these three were forgers. Our suspicion falls on a fourth–not as a counterfeiter, but as a finder and maintainer of these statutes. This is the scholarly, cautious, honorable Munter (b. October 14, 1762, died April 9, 1830), who died in the eighties of the last century in Rome, [where he had the opportunity to explore and study] the papal and other archives [of] history [that the] Church [has]. In the first place, he found all sorts of testimony concerning the Templars, and in the Corsican library, the *Book of Statutes*, the first part of which he published in 1794. He later [gave many] of his papers to Wilcke for his story of the Order of the Temple, while the remainder was destroyed. In a letter to Wilcke from March 17, 1826, he explains that what he had collected about the statutes themselves had been destroyed after use was made of them, and [what we have are] the excerpts of the treatise on the most distinguished ones printed in the *Henkeschen Magazine—Accusations Against the Order*. There is nothing left, however, but some preliminary work on the second part, and some other notes and excerpts from interrogations that you [see] here. Make any use of it [you wish]. However, I do not know how much [of this] you will need, because for 30 years these papers have been lying undetected in my place. As for the accusation of heresy, permit me the counsel to be careful in judging it. When I wrote that treatise, *Henkeschen Magazine* vol. V., I was firmly convinced that the Templars had been orthodox Catholics. But this has since become wavering with me. Their contact with Armenia was easy to associate with Paulicians, and it might well have been that gnostic opinions had crept in with them. "It is now unthinkable and possible that of the statutes in Munter's possession, brought from Rome, which he had destroyed with the other notes and excerpts, [there] had been made a copy, with or without his knowledge before this procedure, and after the long period in which he had not looked at the papers, he no longer exactly focused on these trials and the statutes, but could still recall a vague notion of its content, which seems to elucidate with gnostic opinions from the admonition to caution and from the suggestion of the Templars' connection." Nor was Münter's outward position known, and his connection with Masonic circles [claiming connection to] Christian Templars, which could have been a reason to prevent [the publication of] those secret statutes that are full of heresy? Did not the second part of the statute collection remain unpublished for this reason? It seems to us that an explanation has been found in this way. Whether it is the right one, we must, in the absence of any nearer proof of the fate of the statutes, be left undecided. We can only raise the questions again: Who should have committed a futile forgery? Why should they be faked? Buried under other papers, it could neither harm nor harm anyone, so it missed its purpose altogether.

It is certain that literary deceivers have existed at all times, but their products always had a definite purpose in mind, even if it had only been to enjoy the success of mystification. But there is nothing to be found here. The manuscript went at least 60 years completely unnoticed among other papers and probably even earlier. But, as I have said many a time ago, we dare neither to give judgment on its authenticity nor toward its [fraudulence], and we leave the decision to the church historians, who may express their views. We content ourselves with this strange [thing]–and it remains strange in any case–to have drawn the light of day and submitted it to the scrutiny of criticism.

It is only necessary to remark for a moment that the copy, apparently made in the last half of the last century by a skilled scribe, seems to be an exact copy, except for the few spelling mistakes which we have readily corrected by examining the documents of the Knights Templar statutes indicated as codices XV, XXIV, XXXI, and XXXI [as they were marked] in the Vatican Archives, from which the title–"Monumenta ad disciplinam arcanam fratrum militia Templi"– was ultimately copied, we cannot determine. It is written by the same hand as the whole content, which is why we have retained it. The manuscript apparently–although there is no evidence for it–was passed through Copenhagen, then Stockholm, to Petersburg, and into the hands of the Privy Councilor and Director of Cadet House Böber (died 1819/20), and has no proof of this manuscript with his remaining Masonic legacy. It was confiscated in boxes in Petersburg in the middle of the sixties, but it was then sent to Dr. Buek in Hamburg, emeritus in Physics, who has handed over all these papers to the archives of the great lodge of Hamburg, from which the statutes have been most courteously transmitted to us.

Olderburg

Merzdorf

Monuments to the secret doctrine of the brotherhood the knights of the Temple described in the Vatican Archive.

Order of the poor brothers of Christ and the Solomonic Temple.

Foreword

Above all, our speech is directed to those who despise their own will and wish, in the purity of their soul, to put on the excellent armor of obedience, and to fulfill the desires of the highest and true king with the utmost haste, and to remain [as such]. Therefore, we exhort you, who have hitherto [served] the secular knighthood whose cause is not in Christ, but only in human favor, that you be in a hurry to join those whom the Lord chose from the pit of perdition and with his compassionate kindness for the defense of the holy church united. Above all, whoever you are, you martyrs of Christ, who you choose such a holy conversion, must bring to your conversion the purest care, [and a] firm steadfastness, which is recognized by God as so worthy, holy and sublime when it is lived purely and steadfastly, you appear worthy of a place among the champions who have consecrated their lives to Christ. Thus, indeed, the knightly estate was degenerate and withered, defying the law, not [ministering to] the poor and the churches as was its duty, but proceeding to robbery, plunder, and murder. We are thus shown a benevolence to which the Lord and Savior Jesus Christ has sent his friends from the holy city to France and Burgundy, who for our salvation and the spread of the true faith do not have to sacrifice their lives as a sacrifice acceptable to God.

We find welcome in brotherly love and at the request of Master Hugo, from whom the said cooperative originates, at the mercy of the Holy Spirit from various regions of the ultramontane province on the feast of St. Hilary in 1128 after the impoverishment of the Son of God In the middle of the aforesaid genealogical session, under the guidance of God, they had been convened to hear the order referred to in the individual passages from the mouth of Master Hugo himself, and after recognizing our insignificance, they were the same, only inadequate to us or not worth mentioning for the present council, passing, not reckless, but deliberate of the wisdom and insight of our venerable father Honorius, and of the illustrious Jerusalem patriarch Stephen, a man well-versed in the fertility and needs of the Orient, as well as the poor Comrades of Christ, unanimously recommended in the common chapter. But though most of the Fathers of the Church, who have come together to this council on divine exhortation, have recommended the one we have submitted, it is not to be ignored that I, John of St. Michael, as a scribe whose duty it is to officiate on the orders of the Council and the venerable St. Bernard, Abbot of Clairvaux, in the presence of them honored by divine grace, share their true, unveiled opinions.

First came a Matthaeus, bishop of St. Albano, the Legate of the Holy Roman Church by the grace of God, then Rainald Archbishop of Rheims. The third was Henricus Archbishop of Sens, then the Mitbischoffe, Ranckedus Bishop of Chartres, Goslenus Bishop of Soissons, followed Bishop of Paris, the Bishop of Troyes, the Chairman of Orleans, the Bishop of Auxerre, the Bishop of Meauzc, the Bishop of Chalons, the Bishop of Laudun, the Bishop of Beauvais, the Abbot of Vezelay, who soon afterwards became Archbishop, the Abbot of Cisteaux, the Abbot of Pontigny, the Abbot of Fontaines, the Abbot of St. Denys at Rheims, the Abbot of St. Etienne at Dijon, the Abbot of Molsme; nor was Bernard, the Abbot of Clairvaux, whose opinions were praised by Freimuth, absent. Also present were Master Albericus of Rheims and Master Fulgeriss, among many others, which would be too long to enumerate. Appropriately, the following lovers of truth appear to us as witnesses among the unlearned; the Count Theobald, the Count of Nivernois, and Andrew of Bandinent, [looking their best], [adorned] with the utmost care, softening what appeared inappropriate, [so that they could] thus stood by the Council. The master of the cooperative, by the name of Hugo, did not miss it either, and had some of the brothers with him, for example: Roral, Gaufrid Brisol, Payens of Montdidier, Archembald of St. Amand. The master himself, with his comrades, prescribes the manner and statutes of the humble beginning of his knightly order, the cornerstone of which lies in the saying, "I am the beginning, I who speak to you," to the assembled fathers for information and judgment and, after much consideration of the Scriptures, with the knowledge and approval of the Roman Pontiff and the Jerusalemite Patriarchs, and the attunement of the capitulation of the poor comrades of the Temple in Jerusalem, decided to write them down to oblivion, so that the right Ways to their Creator, whose sweetness surpasses that of honey, which is bitterest compared to Mercy, would be kept inviolate, worthy of conversion, to which they served excellently and could serve through all ages. Amen.

So begins the path of the poor brothers of the Temple in the holy city.

1. How to receive the sacred service.

Those who have renounced their own desires, and others who have dedicated themselves to the service of the Supreme King with the help of weapons and horses for the salvation of souls, should seek the matins and the entire church service according to the Canon Law and the habit of listening to the habit of the learned regulars of the holy city with a pious and pure mind. Therefore, you, venerable brethren, who have despised and praised the light of present life and the maltreatment of your bodies, follow up the disgraceful world of the love of God, refreshed and saturated with divine food, taught and sustained in the commandments of God, after [being enjoined] not to quarrel with the divine mystery, but to be ready to receive the prize.

2. How much to pray Our Lord's Prayer when prevented from attending Sunday service.

If a brother cannot attend the service because he is prevented by the business of oriental Christianity, which will happen quite often, cannot attend the service, we approve and approve that he pray thirteen matins: four for each hora and nine for the vespers. For those who are so busy in the healing ministry cannot go to worship at the appointed hour. If they can attend the service, they are specifically ordered not pass it by.

3. What to do for deceased brothers

When a brother falls dead (and no one is spared from this, since it is always possible to be snatched away); to those chaplains and clerics presently with you who serve the High Priest, we order that you performing the solemn service and Mass to deliver his soul to Christ with care and purity of soul. The brothers, however, ought to give one hundred Lord's Prayers on behalf of the deceased brother until the seventh day, standing there upright and vigilant in prayer for the salvation of their fallen brother. From the first day when the brother's death is to be announced, up to this foretold day, a hundred total prayers should have been completed with brotherly compassion. Of course, we usually receive blessings with divine and most merciful love, and we command this with our pastoral authority. So as the [departed] brother is used to receiving, and is owed, a daily ration of however much food and drink is necessary to sustain life, the board of the departed brother is to be supplied to a chosen poor man to the fortieth day. For we altogether forbid all other offerings (such as the custom in which, in the death of brothers, and in the solemn rite of Easter, and the other sorts of solemn rites, offerings are given to the Master, which is unwise for the Poor Fellow-Soldiers of Christ, who have volunteered for poverty.)

4. The chaplains should only have maintenance and clothing.

Other gifts and alms, which in some way are due to the chaplains or others on a temporary basis in the Order of Weilenden, shall be given to the community of the chapter with the greatest care. The servants of the church should only receive proper maintenance and clothing, and claim nothing further, if the masters do not give them something sweetly and willingly.

5. About the deceased knights, who are at their end.

As there are also knights in the house of God, and in the temple of Solomon, who dwell with us for mercy at times, we plead and implore you out of unspeakable mercy, and strongly order that if the power to be feared prepares the last hour for one of them, a pauper of divine love and brotherly benevolence may hold seven days of prayer in support of his soul.

6. No brother should offer a sacrifice.

We decree, as stated above, that no brother should offer another offering, but remain with his heart, day and night, in his confession, that he may satisfy the wisest of the prophets: "I will receive the cup of salvation, and mine Death mimicking the death of the master; and as Christ gave his life for me, so am I willing to give mine for my brethren. "That is the responsible sacrifice, the living, God-pleasing, gift of redemption.

7. About the immutable standing.

To our ears, the true rumor has come from the undue standing in hearing the service. We do not prescribe this, but reprove it. After the finished song of the psalm: *et venite exultemus Domino* [come and we shall exalt the Lord] you shall all be with jubrity and a song of praise. Healthy as well as sick, be set to avoid annoyance. After a psalm is sung and finished while you are seated, in the "*Gloria patri, etc.*" ["Glory of the Father"] you should rise from your seats in front of the altar to the glory of the Holy Trinity and thus also in the reading of the gospel and in the "*Te Deum laudimus etc.*" ["You we praise, Lord"] and remain during *Laudes* until the decision of *Benedicamus Domino* [We give blessings to the Lord]. That this also happens in the matins of St. Mary is our will.

8. Concerning the feeding of the Convent.

In every palace, or rather, we prefer to say, Refectorium, is to eat collectively and the one who is ignorant of the sign language must inquire quietly and secretly of the one from whom it is necessary to learn something. If, as always, what you need to learn, with submission and humble awe, is more likely to be at table, as the apostle says, "Consume your bread with silence," and the psalmist proclaims: "I have preserved my mouth imposed, ie "I have decided with myself that I will not leave (namely from my tongue) So I guard my mouth so that I do not speak evil."

9. From the lecture.

At breakfast and lunch a sacred lecture should always be held. If we love the Lord, we must desire to listen to His words and commandments with alert attention, and therefore the Reader of the Lection asks you to keep quiet.

10. Of the enjoyment of the flesh.

Three times a week, if not Christmas, Easter, a Marian feast or All Saints Day. Eating meat is enough; for the habit of eating meat is an annoying ruin of the body. If a fast day falls on Tuesday, you should be given plenty on the following day. On Sundays, however, all the brethren, as well as the chaplains, are to be served two dinners in honor of the holy resurrection; the minions and servants receive only one and have to say thanks for it.

11. How the brothers should eat.

Two brothers are usually supposed to eat all meals together, so that one cares for the other, or the harsh way of our life of abstinence does not secretly creep up on one another. But we consider it taken for granted that every knight or brother has an equal measure of wine for himself.

12. Two or three rations of lentils will suffice on other days.

On other days of the week, on Mondays, Wednesdays, and even on Saturday, we keep two or three dishes of lentils or other food (if I may say so, boiled vegetables) for all to observe sufficiently and firmly, so that if he cannot be satiated on one dish, he can eat the other.

13. Which food to enjoy on Friday.

We decreed that on Friday, out of reverence for the Passion of Christ, the whole Congregation (with the exclusion of the sick) be served the food of a fast, from All Saints' Day until Easter, with the exception of Christmas, Marian and apostolic celebrations. At other times, if a general fasting does not occur, it is possible to eat twice.

14. That Grace is to be said after eating.

After breakfast or lunch, we say Grace with a humble heart, always in the church, if it is near, or otherwise in some place that befits our supreme caretaker, Christ. To the servants and the needy, the remnants are to be given with brotherly benevolence (the whole breadth of them).

15. The tithe of bread is to be received by the almsman.

Since the price of poverty, which is the kingdom of heaven, is undoubtedly due to the poor, we command you, who undoubtedly have this belief, that you daily surrender the tithe of the whole bread to your almsman.

16. That the meal is at Master's discretion.

When the sun leaves the east and turns to the west, you have to gather for a complete sign on the given sign, according to the custom and the customs of the area, but before you take the common meal. This meal, however, is subordinated to the insight and discretion of the master, so that, according to his will and command, water or mixed wine is served. But one should beware of overabundance, for we have already seen wise fall.

17. After completing the Complete is silent.

At the end of the Complete, they take to the streets, except, except for emergencies, to observe silence there and quietly [consider] what is to be ordered about the arms-bearers. But should it happen, that at the time of this emergence there would be compelling necessity for a part of the brethren to speak with the master or his deputy, either over a military enterprise or the condition of the house, because at another time they would not have the opportunity to, this is permitted, but we forbid useless talk and antics in this conversation, after the saying "Life and death lies on the tongue," and command the foolish to speak humbly and pure-heartedly say our Lord's Prayer when we go to bed.

18. That the fatigued do not need to get up for Matins.

We decree that weary warriors should not, as you commanded, get up for the Matins, but, with the consent of the Master or the one to whom the Master has delegated their supervision, may rest and be told to pray thirteen paternosters Their sentiments are as if the prophet is saying, "Sing unto the Lord," and "In the presence of the angels I sing to you." But this thing should always be left to the discretion of the Master.

19. That the communion of feeding will always be preserved among the brethren.

In the holy scripture it says, "It was given to each one according to his needs," therefore we do not say that consideration must be given to persons, but only to weakness. If one receives less, thank God and do not be sad; but, because of its weakness, do not rise, and so all the members will live in peace, but we forbid that no one is allowed to surrender to casual abstinence, but admonish that he subordinate himself to the common life.

20. About the style and quality of clothing.

The dresses should be monochromatic, e.g. white or black and be tailored in a double-weave. In the winter and summer, when it is possible, we allow the knights to wear white cloaks, so that they, who have left the dark life, declare themselves bound to their Creator through these bright and white robes. What is the white other than chastity? Chastity is safety of the mind, health of the soul. If the knight does not remain chaste, then he can not attain eternal rest and see God according to the apostle's words: "seek above all for peace, without which no one stands [before] God." But according to our commands, the clothes are without abundance and pride they must be so that everyone can dress and undress themselves. "The drapery has to see to it that everyone is given suitable clothes. When they get new clothes, they should the old in the closet, or where it is otherwise the draper decrees to lay down for the armor bearers, servants or poor.

21. The servants must not wear white smocks.

The bad habit, which was torn in the house of God and its temple-warriors without the permission and consent of the common chapter, we seriously and entirely forbid, and point out that it is a special offense. In the past, the servants and the bearers wore white clothes, which caused unspeakable damage. For in the regions north of the Alps, false brothers, married and others appeared, who professed to be comrades of the temple, though they were worldlings. They caused the knightly order much shame and great displeasure, and the servants, by their exaltation, created a tremendous anguish. They should therefore always wear black clothes; but if they do not live in the province in which they were raised, then they should wear other monochromatic ones [representing] both [locations].

22. Only the knights are allowed to wear white clothes.

No one else, except the aforementioned Knights, is allowed to wear bright coats or white skirts.

23. That one uses the lambskins.

We declare that no brother wears furs, smokes, or the like, which is part of the garment or garment, in the winter, except lamb or sheep's wool.

24. The old clothes are to be distributed among the arms carriers.

The draper should diligently divide the old garments among the arms, servants and arms.

25. Who wants the best, should receive the worse.

If a brother claims the best out of pride, he undoubtedly deserves the least.

26. Consider the size and texture of the dress.

The drapery is obliged to pay attention to the size of the body, and the width of the clothes.

27. The draper observes the equality above all.

The draper, as I have already said, observes the length of the garments so that neither the scoffers nor the prosecutors have anything to complain about, and strive In all to execute God's commandments.

28. The excess of hair.

All the brothers are said to have shaved their hair well so that they can be seen well from the front and back. This is also imperative for the beard, so that neither excess nor reproach of gallantry is made.

29. From beaks and bows.

Beak shoes and bows are known to be used by the worldly, and since this is recognized, we forbid them, and determine, even those who have joined us only temporarily, that no one wears either one. We prohibit beak shoes and bows, superfluous hair and excessive length of the clothes. The Creator [can be found in] inner and outer purity, as expressed in the saying: "be pure in the heart because I am pure."

30. About the number of horses and servicemen.

Each knight is allowed to keep no more than three horses, as the great poverty of the house of God and the Temple of Solomon does not permit to hold at present more without the permission of the master.

31. No one is allowed to beat a vain serviceman.

For the same reason, we grant every knight only one minor; but if any knave should serve a knight for nothing, and out of love, he shall not be allowed to strike him, even from a founded cause.

32. How to take on the followers.

To the knights who serve Jesus Christ and who want to stay in our homes temporarily, those who are ready for such service should buy horses, weapons, and other necessities. We consider it good that the two parties should both negotiate to determine an equitable price. The purchase price should be determined in writing, so that it is not forgotten. That which is necessary to the knight or his horses and knaves, such as the fitting of the horses after use of the house, is to be done by the house with brotherly love. But if the knight loses his horses in the service by some accident, the master shall, if the house can do so, supply others. When he leaves,, the knight himself should pay half of the price, if he so wishes, for the other brethren.

33. That no one conduct himself as according his own will.

To the Knights, who because of the ministry to which they have consecrated and because of Christ the glory of the highest bliss or the fear of hell, the most absolute obedience to the Master is recommended. It is to be carried out in such a way that, without hesitation or procrastination, they immediately follow the orders of the Master or his substitute, as if it were a divine command. Of such is rightly said: "In the call he follows me."

34. When allowed without master's order to go through the city.

Such knights, who have renounced their own will, and others who serve temporarily, we urge in all seriousness that they should not go into the city at night without the permission of the master or his deputy, except to the Holy Sepulcher and the stations which are within the walls of the holy city.

35. Whether allowed to go alone.

No one may be without companions, i.e. a knight or brother, traveling neither day nor night. In the army, no knight, servant, or servant, when they have received lodgings, may bed the lodging of other knights to visit them and speak with them, without orders, as stated above. We therefore confirm what is ordained of God in such a house, that no one will fight or rest alone, but subordinate himself entirely to the orders of the Master, so that he may fulfill the Lord's command: "I have come not to do my will, but to do it Will of the one who sent me."

36. No one is allowed to demand what he needs on the fly.

We prescribe that, because of the erroneous [nature of] desire, this custom is observed most carefully. No brother should demand horse and harness or weapons in a frenzied and challenging manner. Why not? If he is too weak to stand strong any further, or to handle the weight of his weapons, or his horse falls, and this harms the common cause, he shall come before the master or his deputy, and deal with his matter faithfully and clearly. Then the further disposition is at the discretion of the master or the administrator.

37. Concerning bridles and spurs.

We prescribe that neither gold nor silver is needed anywhere on the bridgeheads, shields, and spurs or irons, since it is luxuriant, nor is it permissible for a brother to buy such things. If anyone receives such as a goodwill gift, and it is old, the gold and silver should be colored so that the bright color and the shine do not appear to the others as a sign of exuberance. If such a gift is given and it is new, then the Master should do [with it] so as he pleases.

38. Spears and shields should have no overlays.

It is not permitted to wear suits over shields, lances, spears, and sheaths, because this is no advantage to this, but damage for everyone.

39. About the power of the Master.

The Master is allowed to dispense horses, weapons and whatever else he likes at his discretion.

40. Concerning satchels and bags.

A satchel or bag with a sealable closure will not be allowed. This is to be understood to mean that it is forbidden without the Master's permission, or that of his deputy. But it is not forbidden for the chiefs of the various provinces, nor the Master himself.

41. Of letters.

Never is it permissible for any brother to receive letters from his parents or anyone, nor to answer without the permission of the master or his representative. If he has received such permission, he can read the letter in the presence of the master, if he so wishes. If something is sent directly to him by his parents, he must not accept this until the master has been informed. Also in this regulation neither the master nor the heads of the house are meant.

42. On blurting off fabulations.

Since all useless words are known to be sinful, what will those before the righteous judge say, who boast of their own sins? This is shown to us by the Prophet: "If good talk is silent for the sake of silence, how much more must evil talk about punishment and sin be avoided?" We forbid any brother, or any other member, to defend or to dare tell another about any follies which he so often perpetrated in the state of a worldly knight, especially the carnal enjoyment of miserable women. Whosoever happens to hear the narrator, he shall be silent, and as soon as possible depart and the babbler do not lend his ear.

43. [Regarding] acquisition and acceptance.

If anything is given to a brother through no effort of his own, he shall give it to the Master or trustee. Even if the giver be a friend or a fine father, if the thing is meant only to serve for [the recipient's] own use, he may not accept it without the Master's permission. However, the recipient must not be saddened if the present is due to another, for he must know that he who is angry with it acts against God. However, this directive does not affect the directors, who are particularly responsible for this business, as [the holding of the] pouch or bag has been granted to them.

44. From the food bags of the horses.

To keep this commandment is useful to everyone and should therefore be observed without fail. No brother is allowed to make leinene or woolen feed bags, therefore he should not utilize anything other than perfinell [probably a variety of sackcloth.]

45. That no one seeks to trade or to demand goods.

Now it is not necessary for anyone, brother to brother, to try to exchange things on his own without the permission of the master, or to demand anything that is small, slight, and not of considerable importance.

46. No one should catch birds with birds, nor operate with a bird catcher.

In general, we do not dare to catch a bird with a bumping bird. It is not fitting for a religious [man] to indulge in worldly pleasures, but [rather] to hear the commandments of the Lord, to obey prayers frequently, and to confess his sins to God in tears and sighs. A man who does such a thing and pulls along a hawk or other bird is not allowed to accompany a brother.

47. That no one should shoot with a bow or crossbow.

Since every brother should go along humbly, simply, without laughter, and not speak in many words, but reasonably, and especially [should] not shout out loud, we decree and dispose of every brother to shoot with bows or crossbows in the bush, and command anyone who does the same to go, except [if it be done] with the intention of protecting him from the ungodly Gentiles. Also, he should not scream and rush with the dogs and spur on his horse to hunt wild animals.

48. That the lion is always to hunt.

For it is certain that you are especially advised and commanded to give your life for your brethren, and to destroy the unbelievers, who always threaten the Son of the Virgin from the ground. We have given the lion to you because he goes about looking for whom he devours, and because his hand is against all and all hands against him.

49. In every investigation of you, ye shall hear the judgment.

We know that the persecutors of the holy church are innumerable, and those who do not love the quarrel are continually and cruelly troubled. Hence, the Council, with clear knowledge, has decided that if any one of you in the regions of the East or in any other place should subject [another of you] you to an inquiry, you will hear the judgment given of them by faithful and truthful judges, and what is recognized as right is, inevitably, [what one] should do.

50. That this rule is kept in all its parts.

This rule is–so we command–to be kept in all parts of [regardless of one's] merit.

51. That all knights are allowed to have goods and people.

We believe that after Divine Providence by you in the holy places, this new order began, namely, that you add the knightly to the ecclesiastical, and thus beat the [sin out of the] religious cooperative, armed by the Order. We therefore consider it right that you, who are called fighters of the temple, because of your special merit and as a gift of your righteousness, have land and people, and possess peasants, rule them righteously, and raise from them special tendered gradients.

52. Care must be taken for the sick.

Above all, the greatest concern must be given to the sick brothers, that they should be served Christ, and that the gospel "I was sick and you visited me," should be followed with the utmost care, [or else one will undoubtedly] attain the heavenly retribution.

53. For the weak, the necessary is always enough.

We order the nurses to give the property of the house all their attention and constant care, faithfully and incessantly, to provide meat, poultry, and things like this which can help to restore the patient's health.

54. No one shall provoke anger to others.

It is necessary to prevent one from irritating the other to anger, for the highest love of kinship and divine brotherhood unites the poor and the powerful.

55. How to keep married brothers.

To have married brethren with you, we permit you to follow the following: If they desire the benefits and partisanship of the brotherhood, then both spouses shall leave part of their wealth and whatever they acquire to the common chapter after their death, and until then [must lead] a life of honor and to do good to the brotherhood, but they may not wear white robes. If the man dies earlier, then he shall leave his share to the brothers, and the wife shall keep the other part. But we consider it unjust that such brothers live in a house with chaste women who have become betrothed.

56. The sisters may no longer live in the house of the men.

Sisters living longer with you are dangerous because the old enemy has already driven many out of the way of paradise by dealing with women. Therefore, beloved brethren, we no longer wish for you to persevere in this habit, so that the flower of chastity may always be visible among you.

57. That the temple brothers should not associate with the excommunicated.

That, brothers, is to be avoided and feared! None of the martyrs of Christ is to join an excommunicated or to take care of his things so that he does not fall into the same spell. But when he is banished only from worship, he may treat him and accept his things out of mercy.

58. How to take in secular knights.

If a knight renounces the spoil of ruin or any other worldly aspect of the world, and wishes to be a party to your fellowship and your life, let him not be immediately prompted, but the admittance [shall be as that] according to Paul: "Test the spirits whether they are of God In his presence." The Rule shall be read out, and then, if he promises to live up to the precepts of the Rule, with the permission of the Master and the assembled brethren, in whose presence he expresses his wishes and desires in purity. This is to exempt the time of his trial, at the discretion and wisdom of the Master, in consideration of the solicitude of the requester.

59. Not all brothers are called to the secret assembly.

Not all brothers may be called to the assembly, but only those whom the Master has cautiously recognized as fitting. But if he wishes to negotiate by offering something, such as giving up land to our common religious cause, or to be received by the Order itself, then he may, at his discretion, summon the whole Congregation and, after hearing the opinion of them, perform this action, or offer up something else just as important, or more.

60. One should pray silently.

All brothers should pray standing or sitting, depending on their mind or body, but with due reverence, and not noisily, so that no one disturbs the other while performing their prayers.

61. The servants shall be taken in oath.

We know that many from different regions, both servants and squires, desire with ardent zeal to be admitted to our homes temporarily for the salvation of their souls. It is therefore useful to take them in oath so that the old enemy does not inspire in them anything harmful or inappropriate during their service to God, or even quickly divert them from their good intent.

62. Boys, as long as they are still unexperienced, may not be made temple-brothers.

Although the Rule of the Holy Bakers allows boys to be included in the cooperative, we do not approve of it. Whoever wishes to bring his son or relative into the Order, shall feed him until the years of the manhood, when he can carry arms against the enemies of Christ in the holy land. But then the father or the parents should bring them forth amongst the brothers, according to the rule of the order, so that they may make their decision known. It is better not to [rely upon the] promise of a child, because later as a man [he may] take back the vow.

63. The elderly should be honored.

The ancients are to be respected with pious care for weakness, and treated honorably, and in matters which are necessary to their body, as we are strictly bound in this regard by the Rule of the Order.

64. Of the brothers who travel through the various provinces.

The brethren who are sent to the various provinces shall seek to keep the rule in food, drink, and all other things as far as it is within their power, and to live reproachfully, that they may receive a good testimony from those who stand outside. These commandments of our religion shall not be broken by word or deed, but shall be a good example of wisdom and good deeds to all those with whom they meet. To whomever decides to call upon them, they should be a good host. If possible, the guest-friend's house should not be without light at night, lest the evil enemy find any opportunity to practice evil things which God forbids. When you hear that excommunicated knights are gathering, do not be tempted to go there, and don't think about either gaining temporal advantage or the salvation of their souls. Those brethren who hope to gain access to Outremer shall join the brethren there when they communicate this desire in the presence of the bishop of that province. After hearing his request, the brother should send such a knight to the Master and to the brethren who are in the temple in Jerusalem, where he will be received out of mercy if his life is respectably composed and worthy of such a cooperative, if he seems good to the Master and the brothers. But should he end up dead through hardships, then, like a brother, all the blessings due to a poor comrade of the brotherhood of Christ should be given to him.

65. The food should be distributed evenly.

It is understood, and firmly stated, that all brethren should receive food equally on a local basis, for personal consideration is not useful. But consideration for a [medical] patient is necessary.

66. The temple brothers should have tithing.

Believing that you have forsaken superfluous riches and voluntarily subjected yourself to poverty, we consider it right that you enjoy tithing in the following way. If the Bishop of the Church, to whom tithes are lawfully entrusted, wishes to give you these out of love, then he shall, with the permission of his chapter, communicate the tithing, which is now possessed by the Church. But if a layman wishes to give a tithing, which he has hitherto possessed as his property and possesses to his own detriment, with the permission of the one who presides over the chapter, he can do so.

67. About the heavy and light offenses.

If a brother has committed a slight offense, whether in conversation, in military service, or otherwise, then he should voluntarily report the offense to the Master to receive justice. If there is no traditional penance beyond it, then a slight penitence suffices. But if he has concealed the matter, and it comes to awareness through another, he must submit to the a sharper discipline and greater exhortation. But if the offense is serious, he may be withdrawn from the fellowship of the brethren, so that he may not sit down with them at table, but must take his own food, and submit himself entirely to the consideration and judgment of the Master, that he may saved on the day of judgment.

68. Regarding guilt which a brother does not recognize as such.

Above all it is to be assured that no brother (be he mighty or powerless, an idiot, or weak) who wants to make himself superior and defend his power by defending his offenses, should go unpunished. If he does not want to get better, he may be more severely reprimanded. For he will not be bettered by the pious exhortations and prayers he speaks in his own favor. If in his pride he lifts himself up more and more, then it is necessary for him to be removed from the pious flock, according to the apostle's saying, "expel the wicked man from among you." [*1 Corinthians* 5:13] Then the wretched sheep must be removed from the cooperative of the faithful brothers, the Master holding the rod in his hands, that he might punish the errors of those whom he commands with the right zeal. Otherwise, according to the soulful and carefully deliberated words of the patriarch Maximus, too great a leniency might thereby inspire weakness in otherwise brave men. This is not an overly-strict severity. We must not permit his mistake to persist, so we do not call back the stalkers from the trap.

69. From Easter celebrations to All Saints' Day, linen shirts may be worn.

Because of the great heat of the Orient, we allow out of compassion that, from the feast of Easter to the Blessed Sacrament, every brother who wishes to make use of them can be given linen shirts. This is not done by virtue, but by grace. At all other times, woolen shirts are to be worn.

70. How many and which pieces are necessary for a bed.

We commonly agree and recommend that everyone should sleep alone in his bed, unless necessity, or a matter of the highest importance, requires otherwise. Everyone should have a cot, or bedding, according to the Master's prescription. We trust that a bed-settee, a feather-cushion and a blanket for each man is sufficient. Anyone who does not have one of these pieces should have at least a straw sack and a linen cover sheet of shaggy tissue. They should always sleep dressed in a shirt and trousers. Brothers sleeping together should never forget to keep the lamp burning.

71. Loose talk is to be avoided.

We command you to avoid suspicion, envy, abuse, secret talk, whispers, insults by divine exhortation, and flee from these things like the plague. Therefore, everyone shall eagerly endeavor not to secretly suspect or accuse his brother, but to remember the apostolic saying: "be no accuser amongst people." Have you knowledge that a brother did something wrong? If he does not want to reprove the man himself, he may call in another brother to do so. If the man spurns this, struck with great blindness, and others also suspect him. then he shall be accused in front of all the brothers in a public assembly. Great misfortune comes to those who are not protected from envy, for they will perish due to the wickedness of a skillful enemy.

72. All women's kisses are to be avoided.

We consider it dangerous for any brother to look too much at the faces of women, so we forbid any brother to kiss either a widow, or a virgin, or a mother, or sister, or a friend, or any other woman. The warrior of Christ flees from women's kisses, through which men often endanger themselves, so that with a clear conscience and a strict conduct of life he may always walk in the sight of God. Amen.

This is where the Rule of the Poor Soldiers of the Holy City ends.

New additions to the rule of the Poor Soldiers of the Holy City.

1. That the brothers of the Temple Order should wear a red cross on their mantle.

In the year 1145, under the pope Eugenius, it was first determined that the knights, as well as the servant brothers, should wear on their garments or coats a cross sewn on red cloth, partly in order that this sign differentiate us from the others, and partly because by this we signified the martyrdom, praising [the shedding of] our own blood according to the statutes of our rule to defend the holy land.

2.What banner the brothers should have.

We prescribe that the brethren should have a banner with a cross on a white and black field (*bauceant*), because our friends are as pure and benevolent as Christ, but the enemies are black and terrible.

3. Regarding the seal of the brothers.

Our fathers and co-founders, Master Hugo, and Godfroi of St. Omer, were either so poor or so strict that they both had only one companion. Therefore, as a reminder of their initial poverty, and for the observation of humility, two knights are to be seated on one horse in the coat of arms.

4. About the punishments of perishing brothers.

Since strong fraternity cannot be sustained without discipline, godly and wise men should beware from the beginning, and be prepared for the future. We therefore expressly order and forbid anyone conceal, neglect, or leave unpunished any sort of transgressions by brothers, but rather command them to properly consider the gravity and circumstances of the crime, and to remove any [serious] offender from our cooperative, so that not by defilement with a sick buck is the whole herd of sheep infected, and the Cross blemished. Others, as appropriate to their offense, shall be condemned to eat their little portion of food on the ground without a tablecloth, so that they may be impressed with fear [of further such punishment]. For greater atonement, he should not be allowed to chase away the dogs who want to eat his food. Others still we ordain to be imprisoned for a time before being released, unless it please him to be imprisoned forever in the vessel of Hell.

5. That the brothers owe obedience to the Patriarch of Jerusalem.

We ought to show obedience and veneration to the patriarch of Jerusalem, from whom we derive the origin of our vows and our bodies [our institutions], and give him tithes and other things of God, to do with them whatever the Emperor decides to do.

6. That the brothers are to work.

We strictly order that the brothers should never sit idle or curious when they are not fighting (which, however, seldom happens), so that they do not eat their bread for nothing. When they go about, they should repair the scuffs on weapons, repair garments, or renew old ones, arrange disorderly things, and do all that is the Master's will, and whatever is necessary for the common benefit.

7. How the brothers ought to be bought back from captivity.

If any one of the brothers will be captured in a battle with unbelievers, he should neither wish to, nor ought to, be bought back with the offer of another [captive], and it is preferable that he utilize the supplied girdle and knife so that the captive brother dies in captivity on behalf of Christ, and so that he flies joyously to heaven, than for the man to be brought back to his own men and extend the power of the enemies of Christ.

Here end the new additions to the rules of the Poor Fellow-Soldiers of the Holy City, which I, Brother Mattaeus de Tremelay, wrote as one entry in the year of our Lord 1205 on the day of Saint Felix [January 4th].

2. Here begins the secret statutes which have given the elect to brothers of the temple order as they, the brothers Roger of Montagu, Preceptor of Normandy, and Robert of Barr, procurator of the religious houses there, received them.

1. Of the last times.

Dearest brothers, hear the word of my mouth and receive in your heart what I say to you with the Spirit of God. For the time spoken of by the saints is fulfilled. Repent of your blindness and delusions. The kingdom of God is also close to you, who are baptized not with water but with fire and the Holy Spirit.

2. Of the secret chapters of the Chosen.

If one of you has been chosen Prior, Preceptor, Procurator, Visitator, or Master, he may set up a secret chapter, as appropriate, and put suitable brethren, whom he deems as worthy, into the number of the elect. He must not be omitted from the secret meetings of the elders.

3. About the way to hold a chapter.

The chapter shall be secretly held in the hall, in the rectory, or in the church of the house of the order, either at the beginning of the night, or at the first nocturnal vigil, after the other housemates have been removed from the house and its enclosures, and all at nights, in which chapters be housed outside the house of peace. The Brotherhood of the Chosen gathers to hold the chapter in such a way that it closes all the doors of the house or the church where the chapter is to be held so firmly that no access is permitted, nor that any one else see anything of it or hear what is done in the chapter. A watchman may be placed upon the roof of the house or the church where the chapter is held, so that no one may approach the place where the elect are gathered.

4. How the brothers are called to the secret chapter.

If a secret chapter is to be held, all chosen brethren after the ninth shall be informed by a secret sign of the chapter to be held the next night, from which no one may be excluded, unless death prevents him.

5. Like the brothers who are still attached to the church of Antichrist.

If you have the good opinion of a brother of our order that he should fit into the church of the chosen ones, then you should [receive him] like a wildling who, having been taken to the nursery, will be watered until he has taken root. Then the thorns and superfluous things are discarded, so that a better rice is grafted to it, and cut to the ground, which is later rich in honey-sweet fruit. In the same way, those who are called from the wicked world and Roman Babel in our holy college shall be showered with the waters of fraternal wisdom, until they can awaken and be pruned of the thorns of their offenses with the sword of God, and after removal of the foolish doctrine from their breasts can receive our doctrine, transmitted from the Holy Spirit, in a purified mind.

6.How [to speak to] chosen brothers who continue to be in turmoil.

To a brother whom you know to hear with attentive ears in the manner of a perfect disciple, you may soon be ambiguous, sometimes indignant, now apologetic, soon damning, then again doubting all that which seems fitting to you to speak about the inadequacy of the common rule [and] about the emptiness of the doctrine proclaimed in Babylon, and that if the true Christ of God born of the Virgin Mary was not born and had no true body, he would neither suffer for men, nor would he really lie in the grave, nor could he have been resurrected by the dead. You may add more confidently that in baptism there is no complete purification, nor in the confession which the priest makes, [and no] sacrament [that] the body and blood of the true Christ is contained [in]. At times you may deny the power and necessity of confession and absolution, and let the hearer foresee that in all that the church of Antichrist commands, teaches, decrees, he finds no salvation or truth.

7. What to teach the edited brothers afterwards.

If you notice that a brother who has been so worked on is complaining, despairing and frightened, you may say more confidently to him: "Well, my dear brother, we have all been lying in the maelstrom of false views with the unlearned, until the time came when we started to rise to the top of the true truth, to open our hearts and eyes to the light of the true faith." It is not easy to believe that there are some among us who open to us the gate of salvation, and teach worthiness without hesitation, and the depth of all the true Scriptures, by which we are purged of every blemish of sin and filled with the gifts of the Holy Ghost. We know some who have come from the lands of Outremer, nourished with divine food, and refreshed by inwardness of the soul, as we suppose, see heavenly appearances, because of whose comfort they seem inclined towards nothing [i.e., they are without need], since their God–the one in whom the treasures of wisdom and (heavenly) wealth exist– is always on hand as a companion. If you arouse in this way a repugnance for syncretism and [squelch] their craving for our knowledge, as you will notice, it will be reported on in the next chapter.

8. The despisers of the common rule are not called to the stage of the elect.

Remember, brothers, that you are careful, because it is written, whoever is unfaithful in the least, he will also be unfaithful in the greater. [Do not] invite any brother, regardless of his dexterity, to our union if you know that he, be it from recklessness or out of weakness, has freed himself from, and acted against, the rule of the poor conqueror of the holy city and against the general statutes. It is certain that such transgressors, as unwise, careless and reckless people, should always be kept away from the community of the chosen ones.

9. Brothers inexperienced in the first elements of knowledge are not to be included.

Because ignorance of the beginnings, resulting from enthusiasm, is recognized as the source of most of the delusions, we strictly state that no one from the brotherhood of the temple, from the clerics or laymen (with the exception of the Saracens, who are entirely indifferent to the jargon of the New Babel), to be named among the elect if we have not at least listed them in Trivium and Quadrivium.

10. That Arefast's descendants are not to be included among the elect.

We forbid all descendants of the damned Arefast (Richards of the Count of Normandy Geleitsmann, and even of the Norman Earl dynasty), be they brothers of the temple, clerics, or laymen, to be counted among the brotherhood of the elect, down to the seventh generation.

11. How to take up the brothers.

At a fixed nocturnal hour, clothed as a chosen one and girded with a belt, the brothers gather. After the conclusion of the psalm: "How beautiful are your huts, etc." If he asks who he is, and tells us about what he knows, and his conversion, if the voices of all present [declare him] worthy of admission, the importer, together with two witnesses, is instructed to bring the man into the chapter. In a remote house these three take the same vow, both verbally and in writing, in which he promises, under punishment of eternal prison, and even of death, to keep secret everything that will happen to him until his admission. After the oath is laid bare, he will be led to the door of the chapter, or, if the Receptor would like, behind the altar, and stripped down to his shirt and trousers, one or both, to introduce the candidate and to expose the mouth, the navel, the end of the spine, or even the male member to the witnesses, according to the wishes of the Receptor. Should the candidate refuse to do so, or should he try to do anything indecent in this act, or pretend to do so, or should he betray any doubt, he will be taken to the kitchen or the cellar without further ado, and shall be received with fake ceremonies, such as, for example, having him drink a mixture of vinegar and vermouth, assuring him by such a procedure that he was truly received. One who proves himself to be either ribald or quarrelsome at heart, such a person must never take a place among the elect. But if he has been peaceful, earnest, and efficient, though ashamed, he is to be kissed, and the door of the chapter opened to him, and he is permitted to enter into true reception.

12. What the brother to be included in the chapter has to swear.

After the importer, the witnesses and the candidate enter the chapter, the Receptor thunders with the psalms: "Let God rise up, that his enemies may be scattered," singing choirs in exchange with the brethren down at the feet of the Receptor, with his left hand resting on his chest, his right hand raised to heaven (in the following way, that only the index finger stands outstretched while the remaining fingers are clenched), and swears to observe in inviolable and eternal silence all that he would see and hear in the chapter of the elect, as well as to conceal, deny, and avoid mentioning before any court what is communicated to him by the secret statutes, and swears that he believes and always will believe in God Creator and his indigenous, not-dead, never-dying son, the eternal Word, never born, suffered, crucified, died or risen from the dead. He is finally to swear hate and irrevocable hostility to the worldly tyrants, the synagogue of Antichrist, the new Babel, that is Rome, whose coming John predicted.

13. From the confirmation of the oath.

When the candidate has taken the oath, all the brothers throw the crosses they had in their hands to the ground, kick them, and spit on them. The candidate is encouraged to do this in confirmation of his oath by presenting him with a wooden cross. If he does so without argument, he is received into the number of the chosen ones by the laying on [of hands] of the Receptor and the other brothers, and is then clothed with the costume of the same: a white undergarment made of the finest cloth, and a red belt.

14. Of the despisers of Christ.

If a man, because he saw the wooden crosses trampled underfoot, and he himself did so, then gets the idea to foolishly condemn Jesus, the son of Mary, in his confidential conversations, or to speak mockingly and unworthily of him, we declare him unworthy of the elect and prohibit his further admission to the chapter, except in recordings, and do not allow in any way, be it in whole or in part, for him to gain further knowledge of the secret ordinances. For no one who is spiritually of God [would] say "Jesus be damned," and no one can say, "Jesus, the Lord," except in the sense in which he has been revealed to us by the Holy Spirit.

15. Prohibition of the publication of the articles of association, conclusion of the chapter and various types of recording.

It is strictly forbidden to translate the secret statutes into one's national language, or into any other foreign language, or to read the same into recording chapters, or to impart them to brothers so that they may read them outside of the chapter. We do not want a chapter Visitator to come on the third Vigil of the night and for the Prior or Master to order it to be closed. The Praeceptor shall say "Go, and do not throw the saint before the dogs and your pearls before sows, so they do not turn against you and tear you apart. In the freedom which that true deity of God has earned you, never abiding in the bonds of bondage. (Here he stretches out his hand to heaven). May the God of all joy and peace fill you with confidence in the faith, that you may be filled with the hope and the strength of the Holy Spirit." With his hands outstretched against the brethren, he shall bless them without the sign of the cross, saying, "God of wisdom, God of light, God of peace be with you all, amen!" Then the brothers depart in profound silence. The following words are used everywhere by the Praeceptor: "We bend our knees to the Father of all in heaven and on earth (laying his hand on the head of the candidate), who strengthens you in virtue according to the riches of his grace through his spirit within man, that the true Christ may live in your heart by faith, strengthened and sustained by love, so that you may, along with all the chosen and saints, understand what breadth and length, height and depth it is to experience the excellent knowledge and love of the true Christ, so that you may weep with God's fullness." The same is repeated by the chaplain, while the brothers sing with one hand raised towards the candidate. In addition to these particular uses, every Preceptor, Prior, Visitator, Procurator, or Master is not only free, but is even required, to add and use various observances, customs, ordinances, and ceremonies for admission in his chapter, so that by using them diversely, we would more securely conceal our secrets from the world and from maleficent spies.

16. How many times in the year the secret statutes are revealed to the brothers.

We prescribe the celebration of four vigils, namely to celebrate Fridays and, annually, the days of Epiphany, St. John the Baptist, and the Archangel Michael. In the chapters to be held on those nights, no recordings may be made, but the secret statutes only are to be presented to the brothers and, if necessary, new regulations are declared, arising disputes are settled, and quarrels both domestic and larger are carefully settled among the secret cooperative.

17. Law and Doctrine of the Chosen.

But know, ye chosen brethren, that our law and doctrine, which we have received from our fathers and masters in Outremer, was not invented contrary to the commandments of the gospel nor to the apostolic statutes, for it is the following: to renounce the world, to curb the cravings of the flesh, to hound thieves, usurers, slanderers, fornicators, and robbers, by labor, be it with the hands or with the spirit, to seek one's subsistence, not to harm a good man, to embrace all who are zealous for our knowledge, and to obey God more than man. If we abide by these principles, it is not necessary for the sacraments which are offered in the synagogue of Antichrist; but if we violate them, those sacraments cannot contribute to our salvation. This is the sum of our justification, to which the use of new ceremonies is unable to add anything, since every apostolic and evangelical doctrine concludes with it.

18. About the synagogue of Antichrist.

Remember, dearest brothers, to let no one seduce you, for now there are many who say, "We are Christ's, and profess Christ," but they lie, proclaiming Antichrist and denying the true Christ through a life tainted with sins. Therefore, remember that the kingdom of God is not in the words of dogma, but in virtue; that it is not eating and drinking that is the kingdom of God, but righteousness, peace and joy in the Holy Spirit, and that the kingdom of God does not come from observations of outward things, and that those who say, "behold, here it is, behold it," lie, for the kingdom of God is in you. Therefore, take it for granted that the Church of the true Christ transformed into the synagogue of Antichrist in the time of Pope Sylvester, and that Peter's Rome had been redesigned into New Babel, the city of Baal. From there come those, formerly Pharisees, now false prophets in the people, and those lying-masters who sit on the chairs and in the councils, and bring in rulers from the hill who bought them, and deny God. In spite of their statutes, the commandment of God remains undefeated, for they teach only the opinions and orders of men, and confess with their lips, blindly and as leaders of the blind, about God, from whom their hearts are far removed. Everywhere you see them, dragging heavy and unbearable burdens together and throwing them upon the shoulders of men, yet not wanting to move a finger, as they do their works so that they are seen by men, purporting to shut some men out of the kingdom of God, into which they themselves do not enter, or to let others in. They pervade the sea and the land, holding long speeches to make a proselyte, whom they have made, if they have converted him, the son of condemnation, though they indeed are twice as damned as you are yourself. They are in all whitewashed tombs, which appear to men as righteous from the outside, but inside are full of hypocrisy and injustice. They know how to build the tombs of the martyrs and erect the monuments of the saints, but they persecute every saint and make a marty of anyone who, in their opinion, speaks contrary to God's commandments.

19. At the mercy of the chosen ones.

It is written: "I have selected seven thousand men who did not bow their knees before Baal." Thus, in these last days, too, the remnants have been taken up to grace after selection. They were lifted up, but the others were robbed of their eyes, as it is written, "God gave them the spirit as a punishment, eyes, lest they see, ears, lest they should hear till this day." Even over us the night of darkness had come, but the day of selection came. Let us therefore throw away the works of darkness which we have done in the synagogue of Antichrist, and clothe ourselves with the weapons of light, and let us be a body and a soul, called in the invitation of hope by Faith, a baptism of the Spirit, a God and Father of all, who is above us all and through us all and in all of us.

20. From the faith of the chosen ones.

Since you are the chosen race, the royal priesthood, the holy congregation, the people of property, in which there are neither Jews nor free, neither Romans nor Saracens, neither man nor woman, for you are all one in that true divinity; We proclaim to you a God who has revealed himself through this world and through everything in the same in which we live, weave and are. We also proclaim to you the indigenous Son of God, that true Christ who was in and with God from eternity, who could never be born, nor suffer, nor die, to whom all things visible and invisible are given in heaven and on earth, the one Son of Mary whose Soul was alive and thus in the world, but the world did not recognize him, because the animal people did not understand what the Spirit was. Of Jesus, the true son of Joseph and Mary, we assert that all that he taught was sacred, and that the miracles which he performed, he did only by virtue of the power of that true Christ who from eternity was an outflow of God himself temporarily united with the soul of Jesus, but never physically appeared. But because the Son of Mary was righteous and holy and was not part of any sin, we worship him in God and pray to him, but we consider the wood of the cross to be the sign and symbol of the animal of which you read in Revelation , and for a desecration of the sanctuary. Incidentally, we who have written the law of the Holy Spirit in our breasts, are neither eager for the earthly, nor do we believe the [words] of carnal-minded men written on animal skins. For as we know that many a speech of the holy prophets was inspired by the Spirit of God, and some by the evil spirit of this world, we follow the admonition of the apostle: "Test everything, keep the good."

21. The freedom of the chosen.

If you, O brethren, are led by the Spirit, as the Spirit of God lives in you, then you are no longer under the law, but under grace. The fruits of the Spirit are love, joy, peace, patience, benevolence, goodness, forbearance, gentleness, faith, humility, austerity, and chastity, which is not founded in the law, but the opposite. Delivered from the bonds of death in which you lie, serving in renewal of the Spirit and in the ancient faith of Scripture. Before you were elected to the freedom that was revealed to you, you were caught up in the law. Therefore that law was your disciplinarian in Christ, that you might be justified and chosen by it. But if you choose, you are no longer under the disciplinarian, but have received the freedom of the sons of God. Now that you have recognized God and have known God, do not turn to the feeble and wretched beginnings of the Law and the Synagogue of Antichrist to further serve with your heart.

22. From fasting.

Therefore, we release you from any fasting command, but without offending the weak and those who are not among you. No one may condemn you for food and drink; everything is pure to the pure; There is nothing clean about the polluted and the unfaithful, because their soul and conscience are in unfairness. You can eat of everything that comes to the meatbasket, according to your conscience, asking no one, for the earth and its fullness is the Lord's.

23. On the Traffic of the Chosen with the Unbelievers.

If invited by a Jew or Saracen (who condemns the new Babylon as unbelievers) to a table, and you accept the invitation, eat all that is presented, and despise those who, as the Spirit clearly predicted, believe that this is being unfaithful to God, following the spirits of error and the teachings of evil spirits with hypocritical falsehoods and branding in their conscience. Avoid those who forbid the food God has created with thanksgiving, since all God's creation is good to the faithful, and to them who know the truth.

24. Of the journeys of the chosen ones.

Those who serve in the field, be it to the Orient or to Spain, must wage war justly and mildly, defend only the oppressed and punish the wrongdoers, but indulge as little as possible in your lust for glory, or even the princes' lust for dominion, or even that which would be most ignominious- to go out to prey. You should remember–whether in open-field battle, or in [the state of] truce or [in the process of] peacemaking–that your God is also the God of the Jews and Saracens, and that it is more often pleasing to God [to protect their] rights than the righteousness of those who abuse the virtue of our holy order, more attached to the hypocrisy [that issues from the tongues of popes] under the pretext of Christianity, and who seek more for the glory of their [own] power than for divine glory. We approve that in all of our congregations, where you know more or less Brothers Chosen, you will spend some time in multiplying or spreading the light of your election through diligent conversation. We also exhort you, as many sons of our fathers are scattered in different parts of the world, and are charged with various business and trades, that you seek to find them through the signs entrusted to you. When one of you comes to the city of Orleans, he shall make a humble pilgrimage with ten sons of our fathers, whom we have received, to the court outside the city wall, where the glorious martyrs of divine science, the bishops Stephen and Lisojus, who were burned on the orders of King Robert, and should [therein] celebrate their memory. That is why we pray to God most urgently.

25. Observation of the general rule and of confession.

Do not believe that you are chosen and sent to abrogate the commandments, be it the rule of our order, or the rule of the synagogue. On the contrary, you must believe that you are chosen and sent to fulfill them in the eyes of men, so that there will not be anger towards you. Therefore observe strictly our common rule, as well as the Roman statutes and habits; but worship in your spirit no other law than that which is written in your hearts by the Holy Ghost. Therefore, if conscience accuses one of us of transgression of this law, he will confess, but no one else but a brother is chosen by him as a priest or a layman, remembering the Tertullian saying: "Are we laymen not also priests?" It is written: "We too have been chosen as the priesthood of God the Father" (the ecclesiastical power has defined the difference between priests and laity), therefore you can read and baptize Mass and be yourself a priest, even if you are not a member of the spiritual profession. Where there are three, albeit lay people, there is church, for everyone lives by and in his faith. Therefore, if you have the priestly right within you, then you must also possess priestly power when necessary.

26. The right of the Chosen in the government of houses.

In the individual houses and lodgings, where at least two or three brothers are chosen, they shall endeavor, with careful zeal, to bring to the heads and administrators only the chosen brethren, whether by election or proposal. With just such wisdom, you brothers should keep chosen ones together in the general chapters in the election of visitators, preceptors, procurators, and other superiors (excluding the Grand Master).

27. On the construction of workshops and other secret facilities.

If one of the chosen electors has received the office of a prefect, he should eagerly see too it that the workshop of the house be arranged as soon as possible, for which he will seek the assistance and art of such master masons whom he has recognized as a descendant of our fathers, as our secret customs require. If he is still a stranger, he may, if he is clever, reveal to him the light of the election. But then may he hurry to set up the secret chapter of the elect, so that by his wise service, the light of God will soon dispel the darkness of the synagogue of Antichrist. We prescribe that the chaplain of the house of the elect shall be made docile and graceful in all things, and if he remains obstinate, and proves himself completely unworthy, chase him away, and summon another. The appointed chaplain may go so far as to admonish the brethren, both the knights and armies and servants, to confess their sham confession remorsefully, like other clergymen, to the chairman of the house, because he has the power to acquit them and to remove all sins from them, both the known and the secret. If any doubt arises, you must assert that such privilege has been conferred upon the leaders of the temple-masters by Christ (by which you tacitly mean our supreme high priest, that true Son of God).

28. Of libraries and studies.

We demand, dear brothers, that you use the utmost care to establish libraries in your homes, and exhort you to keep, besides the scriptures and the works of the Holy Fathers, the master of the unification of nature Atto of Vercelli's *The Book of Ecclesiastical Printings* [*The Vercelli Book,* Old English poetic codices], the *Monologium* and *Proslogium* of the master Anselm of Canterbury, Peter Abaillard's books of theology [*Theologia Summi Boni,Theologia Christiana,* and *Theologia Scholarium*] and the [collection] of opinions *Sic et Non,* Gratian's concurrence of inconsistent statutes [*Concordantia discordantium canonum, or The Canon of Discord and Concord],* the master Petrus Lombardus books of opinions [*The Sentences, Books 1-4*], the Master Gilbert Porretani's book of the Trinity [*De Trinitate*], John of Salisbury's *Policraticus* and *Metalogicus,* and finally those writings which these days have been condemned by the Pharisees of the synagogue, such as the divine writings of the master Amalric de Bena and David of Dinant, from which you can draw for your treasury, never letting your houses lack resources of wisdom. So that you should not be regarded as inexperienced the courtly tongue when dwelling in the courts of princes, bishops, or court-chairs, we most seriously prescribe that you should devote yourself to the study of decrees and laws.

29. Of the betrayal and swearing.

If one is found to have betrayed even the slightest of the secret statutes, the signs, or of what is being discussed in the nocturnal chapters, out of recklessness or talkativeness, then he shall in time, according to the magnitude of his offense, serve his punishment in chains and never be allowed to continue to attend the chapters. But when it is known that he has committed treachery in the corruption of his heart, he shall be kept in perpetual imprisonment, or, if the common good seems to require it, punished with secret death. But if you are summoned before any court and questioned about the laws, usages, statutes, and secret business, then you should bravely resist such a tyranny by denying it, and denying it again, and even pleading your ignorance with firm courage, certainly that the Accusation of perjury and its insult before God does not fall on you, but on the shameful investigators, but that you will receive the reward of truth not revealed.

30. Of the death and burial of the elect.

If one of you becomes dangerously ill, it is our commandment that one of the brothers should always stand by the patient and not leave him alone for a single moment. But if, by chance, there is not a brother who is a chosen one in this house or its realm, then the patient himself should cause one to come from the next house. If, however, the dying man should be frightened with remorse for any cause, the chosen brother should reassure him and endeavor in every way for the peace of his soul, by hearing confession from him and absolving him of all sins, whatever their nature may be. On no account may it be conceded that anyone who is frightened by the power of the disease may speak alone to any brother, be it a cleric or a layman who is not one of the chosen. The deceased brothers are to be buried with their red belt, and in their exequies the Mass of the Holy Spirit is to be administered in a red robe, but on the tombstone shall be the Pentalpha, the oldest sign of salvation.

Here ends the secret statutes, narrated by the brothers Roger of Montagu and Robert Barris, written off by me, the brother Bernard of St. Omer, in the fifty-second light of the twelfth century XV.[1315] Cal. August.

3. Here begins book of the baptism of fire [*Consolamentum*], or the book of the secret statutes, which Master F. Roncelius has written down for the consoled brothers of the Temple Militants.

1. Concerning the light of baptism of fire [*Consolamentum*].

The people, who were walking in the dark, see a great light, and a light has risen for those residing in the shadow of death. We also see this light, for we mourned and were comforted, and in the fear of bondage, freed from the Spirit, we received the spirit of adopted sons, in which we cry: one is our Father, Master, Redeemer, Consoler, God, and his spirit gave to our spirits the testimony that we were children of God.

2. Concerning the adherence of the consoled brothers.

Dear brothers, who have ears to hear, notice! You are given to recognize the secrets of the kingdom of God. Blessed therefore are our eyes that see, and your ears that hear. Know that kings, popes, bishops, abbots, and magisters have wished to see much that you see, but they have not seen, nor do they see, and hear what you have heard, but they have not heard, nor hear.

3. Concerning the true religion.

We proclaim to you, brethren, that the hour has come when neither on the mountain here nor there, neither in Jerusalem nor in Rome, is the Father to be worshiped. The Spirit is God, and if you are of God, you must worship him in spirit and in truth. Remember that all which Jesus spoke through this true Christ is the spirit and life of God; for the Spirit and life are of God; therefore it is the spirit of God which makes one alive. The flesh of Jesus is not not able to profit anyone.

4. Concerning the mystery of the consoled.

God is love, and whoever stays in love stays in God and God in him. We speak to you of the wisdom of God in secret, which is hidden from the children of New Babylon, but which God has predetermined to be revealed to our fathers through humble workmen in brick and mortar, they which gave to us, and to their sons, glory and salvation. None of the princes and high priests of that time knew you, for if they had ever known them, they would never have worshiped the wood and the sign of the cross, nor would they have lead those who harbor the spirit of the true Christ to the stake.

5. Concerning the love of the consoled to all.

But in the field of truth, ye saints and citizens of the household of the house and temple of God, established upon the ground of the wise by the saints of yore, remember that before God there is no respect of personage. Unrest and anxiety are an evil to the soul of every man who works for him. This is the same for every man, be he Christian or Jew, Greek or even Saracen. But glory, honor and peace be unto all who work for good: to the Jew and to the Christian, to the Saracen no less than to the Greek. For you, therefore, in love there is no difference between a Jew, a Greek, a Roman, a Saracen, a Franconian or a Bulgarian, for each [have] the same Lord, who enriches all who call upon him; anyone who calls on the name of the Lord will be saved.

6. Of the external conduct of the consoled.

Since you are free from every yoke of bondage which enthralls the children of New Babylon, charmed by the spirit of the worst dogmas, you must assign yourself as a servant to all, so that you may deliver the elect into the light and freedom. Therefore, appear to the Jews as Jews and to the Saracens as Saracens, so that you may win over Jews and Saracens. To those who are under the law of New Babylon, may it appear as if you are likewise under the same law, though you are exempted from it by the election and the baptism of fire [*consolamentum*], that you may set free those who are bound by the laws of New Babylon. May you be all so that you may save all. But be cautious about all [matters concerning] the eternal gospel of the one God, so that you may fully share it, avoiding all zeal that is not pursuant to wisdom, so that you will never provoke offense or anger, be it from the Jews, the Saracens, or the citizens of the kingdom of God, or even the servants of New Babylon.

7. Concerning the wisdom of the consoled.

Know, dearest brothers, that because all who love God must do all things in the name of good, and you who are called according to the will are sacred, therefore for you everything is allowed, but not all things are expedient. Therefore, be wise as serpents and gentle as doves, betray nothing of the baptism of fire [*consolamentum*] to babblers who care not for our light, nor shall you reveal anything of our science to the scantily-minded or feeble-minded, who can not understand it, nor contradict them in their foolish views, but touch upon these things only softly, so that they awaken staggering, blinking their eyes, and seeking a guide, demand our guidance. Yes, we earnestly insist that you take care that the common rule is closely observed in your homes, and that you, everywhere in the household, do nothing contrary to the customs, statutes, and laws of New Babylon, or even despise them but, rather, consider this as such with the beginnings of boys, who at first are unable to tolerate strong food but soon are able to mature and be invigorated by it. But in order to be able to exercise the secret customs of our baptism [*consolamentum*] more surely and more profitably, make sure that in every house, dwelling place, and place where you hold the chapter, sufficient chambers are made with secret entrances outside the house or dwellings leading to underground accesses, so that the men of all estates, orders, parties, can come to your nighttime meetings without arising the suspicions of the resident brothers based on preconceived notions.

8. Of those who can be admitted to the nighttime chapters of the baptized [*consolati*].

We exhort you therefore, brethren, that you faithfully entertain the communion of the saints, because the saints are scattered throughout all the regions of the earth, that the mysteries of the kingdom of God may be expressed from sunrise to sunset. As you wander through locales near and far, you will find the righteous among all peoples, bearing in their hearts the grace of our election and the light of our baptism of fire [*consolationem*]. They belong to us and never left us. Therefore, if you see large buildings, approach the masters of masonry assembled for such work and question them by the secret signs. You will then learn that many of them are familiar with the knowledge of God and the great art; they have received both from their fathers and masters, from whom we too have received them; they above all are our brothers, as well as those men in the province of Toulouse who call themselves "Good people" [Cathars] and the poor of Lyons [Waldensians], and the Albigensians, who live in secret between Verona and Bergamo, and the Bagnolensians in the province of Galicia and in Etruria, and the Bogomils of Bulgaria. Therefore, it is yours, and it is also for your benefit, for us to admit those from these brotherhoods who have proven themselves through their achievement of the highest peak of knowledge, into our nighttime chapters through the underground passages, but those who, out of fear of spying pursuers, are prevented from full knowledge in their meetings, you should, if you have otherwise recognized them as worthy, bestow either the grace of election or the light of the baptism of fire [*consolamentum*], or both, outside the chapter in the presence of three baptized [*consolati*].

9. Concerning hospitality.

If by chance some of the above-mentioned fraternities come to your homes, places of residence, or squares, then we want and prescribe, above all, that you receive them lovingly and as brothers, and provide for them all of life's comforts that are available, and then you will know the things suitable to put your own spirits at ease; join them and take part if they want to work their sacred practices in your underground chambers. We prescribe the same to those baptized [*consolati*] brothers who are in Cyprus or Spain, if either the Saracens or the Druze, who hide in the mountains of Lebanon, come to them seeking an offer of hospitality and if they desire to worship, according to their faith, God the Father of all among our brethren. Nor do we deny the brethren baptized of those regions, Saracens and Druze, in which the Spirit of God works, and which are worthily found to be part of the elect and to participate in the baptism of fire, assisted by three brothers outside of the chapter. It is worth recalling the strange and striking example of this being given by Brother Honfrid of Tours to Saladin.

10. How to deal with resident brothers.

We decree that not one of the resident brethren should be admitted before the end of the thirty-fifth year of his life, and only when he has evinced the ripe fruits of his election, and has proved himself well-versed in the decree.

11. As with the monks, clerics, abbots, etc.

We place the greatest caution on you against monks, priests, pastors, bishops and masters of science, however. Ye shall not hastily establish such company, for they act deceitfully, brooding treason in their hearts, and yet they seek the light, having renounced the precedent of their sins–they who so freely plunged themselves into filth and scandal. Therefore, those who seem to be better than this, though you may have studied and observed them for a long time, should not be received in the chapter, but rather in some dwelling place in the presence of two or three brothers. But do not tell them about the statutes and customs. After many years of uninterrupted conversations and unequivocal examinations, and then only, should such a one be introduced to the chapter as a member.

12. As with the laity.

The lesser part of the anxieties and risks for you will be with the laity, who serve God either through the court of princes or by means of their possession in the simplicity of their hearts and in their honest way of life, and give justice and fairness to men. Those who have proven themselves to you and who, awakened by your wisdom, desire to receive grace and light, should first be joined with you as brother comrades, then take the precaution not to include them in the chapter among the elect, or to place them among the number of the baptized [*consolati*], even if they have remained steadfastly good.

13. How the baptism of fire [*Consolamentum*] is performed in the chapter.

Every elect brother, before receiving the baptism of fire [*Consolamentum*], must give his preceptor in writing a general and complete confession of all his crimes and crimes which he has committed from the time he reaches the years of distinction to the present day and confirm the truth and completeness of this confession in the presence of two witnesses. The document is kept in the archives of the chapter. The Master, Prior, Preceptor, Visitator or whoever else accompanies the office of the Receptor, opens the chapter with the antiphony: "This commandment," then he begins to sing the psalm: "Lord you study me and know me" and the brothers sing the whole song in choral exchanges. After completing the psalm, the the Receptor speaks the whole antiphony (Deuteronomy, Chapter 30, 11-17 [truncated]): "This commandment, that I command thee this day is not above thee, nor far off from thee: Nor is it in heaven, nor is it beyond the sea. But the word is very nigh unto thee, in thy mouth and in thy heart, that thou mayst do it, that thou mayst love the Lord thy God, and walk in his ways, and keep his commandments and ceremonies and judgments, and thou mayst live, and he may bless thee in the land, which thou shalt go in to possess." Immediately at the beginning of the antiphony, the elect brother is led into the chapter, and placed in the midst of it. After the antiphony, all the baptized brothers lay their hands on the new brother, indeed swearing secrecy, faithfulness, and inviolable obedience. The Receptor releases him from all sins, as well as from all the laws, commandments, customs, and doctrines of New Babylon, in the name of the one and only God, the eternal, who is not born yet is born, in the name of the true Christ, who has not died and neither will die. Then the three prayers of the three prophets sent by God concerning the baptized are spoken of by the brethren, the first of whom stands upright with him, holding his hands over his head, the second kneeling with his hands and arms outstretched, with the third prostrating his whole body and face to the floor.

14. The prayer of Moses.

The first prayer is that of Moses and reads as follows: "Let their the strength of the Lord be magnified, as thou hast sworn, saying: The Lord is patient and full of mercy, taking away iniquity and wickedness, and leaving no man clear, who visitest the sins of the fathers upon the children unto the third and fourth generation. Forgive, I beseech thee, the sins of this people, according to the greatness of thy mercy, as thou hast been merciful to them from their going out of Egypt unto this place [for] the baptism of fire [*consolamentionem*] and your light; Have mercy on us. Amen." [This is a quote from *Numbers* 14:17-20, up to the term "baptism of fire."] To which the Receptor answers, "And the Lord said, as I live, so shall all the world of the glory of the Lord be filled." [This is quoted from *Numbers* 14:21.] Immediately, the Introductor approaches the elect brother and cuts off some of the hair, some of the beard, and some of the nail of the index finger of his right hand, saying, "Serve God, rather that you be circumcised of the heart than of the flesh in the sign of the everlasting covenant between God and the spirit of men. Amen."

15. The prayer of the Son of Mary, called Jesus.

The second prayer, to the true Son of Mary, we speak as follows: "Eternal Father, glorify us with yourself, with the glory that we had with you before this world was. We have revealed your name to the people, who you have given us from the world. They were yours and you gave them to us, and they kept your word, and they know that all that you have given us is from you. Holy Father, keep them in your name, which you have given us, and receive this our brother, whom we have chosen in your name, to be one with you, just as we are. We have given your word to him and the world hates him. He is not of this world, as we are not of the world. Sanctify him in your truth; your word is the truth. Righteous father, the world does not know you, but we know you, and he recognizes this because you have sent us and we announce your name to him, and declare that love, that you have loved us [with], is in him and we in him. Have mercy on us. Amen." (*John*, Chapter 14.) [As noted, this last line seems inspired by the part in the fourteenth chapter of *The Gospel of*

John, verse 11, where Jesus asks his disciples, "Believe you not that I am in the Father, and the Father in me?" After completing the prayer, the Receptor says: "There came a voice from heaven [, saying] : this is my dear son, in whom I am well pleased!" [This line comes from an event said to have occurred during the baptism of Jesus by John, recounted in *Matthew* 3:17, *Matthew* 17: 5 and *Luke* 3:22.] Then the Introductor puts a ring on the right index finger of the brother, saying: "Son of God, take this ring as a sign and a pledge of your eternal union with God, the truth and us! Amen."

16. The prayer of Baphomet.

As a third prayer we approve of Baphomet, which reads: "In the name of God, the gracious and merciful, we thank God, the Lord of the universe, the gracious and merciful, the Judge of the Day of Judgment. We worship you, we trust you, you send us on the right path, the way of those who have chosen you, not on the path of those whom you are angry with, nor on the path off the unfaithful ones. Also guide him our faithful brother to the right target, to the goal of those, I say, who are pleasing to you and against whom you are without anger, and he will not err. O God, having returned to you, we follow your command, expect forgiveness, and ask that you do not wish to take vengeance for the sake of our forgetfulness and error. You, God, a giver of forgiveness, will be gracious and kind to us, you who are our Lord. Amen." At this, the Receptor adds, "One Lord, one faith, one baptism, one God and Father of all, and everyone who invokes the name of God will be saved." Now the Introductor raises the brother to the elect, and anoints his eyelids with holy oil, saying, "I anoint thee a friend of God with the ointment of grace, that ye may see the light of our baptism of fire [*consolamentum*] shining for you and us all, in the way, truth, and eternal life. Amen."

17. About the unveiling of the idol.

Having done so, the Receptor takes the idol Baphomet out of his box and shows it to the brothers with his hands raised, saying, "The people that walked in darkness saw a great light, and the light has risen for those who were in this region and sat in the shadow of death. There are three who testified of God to the world, and these three are one." All the brothers call out, "Yah-Allah," that is, "the glory of God." Now all the brothers come to the Receptor one by one, kiss the idol and touch it with their girdle, and finally the elect brother may do the same, and then the Receptor grasps both hands and raises them, saying, "Now the Son of man is praised, and God is glorified in him. Behold brethren, a new one, a Friend of God, who then speaks, however much he may want, with God, to whom you ought to give thanks, because he has led you to that place you have desired much and he fulfilled your wish. Let God's glory remain in the heart and spirit of all of us, Amen." After these words, he dismisses [the newly-elected brother] and begins to sing the praise of wisdom (*Ecclesiasticus* Chapter 24) at the end of the chapter, which the brothers continue to the end in choral exchanges.

18. The completion of the baptism of fire [*Consolamentum*].

At the end of the chapter [from *Ecclesiasticus*], the Receptor will take the newly-baptized to the hall of records that night or another, and there show him the secret science of God, the sonship of God, of Jesus and the true Baphomet, of New Babylon, the nature of things and eternal life, also to the secret arts of man, of great philosophy, of Abrac and talismans, be it in its whole extent or only in parts, as it appears useful and certain. We wish and demand this completion of the baptism of fire, as well as the knowledge of the signs, be withheld as long as possible from the accepted clergy, monks, ministers, bishops, and masters of science.

19. Concerning the practice of arts.

But we expressly command, and dictate, that in houses where every single resident brother is not elect or baptized [*consolati*], certain matters should not be worked upon by philosophical art, e.g. to take imperfect metals of their own element and to transmute them into true gold and silver by said art. But if adepts want some of this art to be worked, they are only able to do this for themselves in distant houses, under the greatest discretion and for the benefit of the baptized [*consolati*].

20. Concerning elections.

Our advisory forbids, under threat of death, that any baptized brother to be elected Grand Master of the Knights Templar, or allow his election, or, if chosen, to assume office. However, baptized brothers, if they are attending the elections, should choose themselves, or cause themselves to be chosen, as candidates for the positions of visiting inspector, home procurator, preceptor, or prior.

Here ends the book of baptism of fire [*Consolamentum*] or the secret statutes, which have been put together by the master Br. Roncelinus in a book. I have signed it off, I, brother Robert of Samford, Procurator of the Templar houses in England in the fortieth year of the light after the thousandth two hundredth IV [1204]. Cal. Jul.

4. Here begins the registration of the secret signs, which Master F. Roncelinus has put together.

1. You will incidentally ask a brother Templar coming from wherever, who seems to you to know something higher: "What is the origin of the light?" And if he answers: "The night!" Then he is elect. And if you ask further, "What happened around the ninth hour?" and he answers: "it is completed!"–then he has seen the light of baptism of fire [*consolamentum*].

2. If a master mason does not seem to be an ordinary man, ask him: "Where does the light of your craft come from?" If he answers: "From Abrac!"–he is a son of our fathers and our brother.

3. If you suspect that a monk or abbot is one one of us, or may be as like one cast by us, ask him: "Who is your mother and who is your brother?" and if he answers: "They who do the will of my father!"–hold him to be your brother.

4. If you believe that a clergyman, be it a priest or bishop or master of the sciences, aspires to the same higher things, ask him: "Where is your temple?" If he answers, "The Lord is the earth and the fullness of it!"–you will regard him to be not without some light of our science.

5. When you come together with any layman and suspect mystery is in him, whisper in his right ear: "Peace to you!" If he answers: "Peace in God!"–believe that he is elect.

6. At times, even the weakness of women, be it in the lay or spiritual garments, will send across rays of divine light into your eyes. From such you shall ask by silence: "Say good, what is your glory?" If she answers with downcast eyes: "The lamp filled with oil for the arrival of the bridegroom!"–ye shall honor your sister in her.

7. And if any of the Saracens, who comes to you or meets you in street shows special respectability, ask him: "Is the seed of the purple-leaf plum sown in your city?" If he answers: "It is sown in the

heart of the faithful!"–he is one of the Druze, and is not to be treated as a foreigner, but received with honor.

8. Besides these, it is also necessary to diligently learn those signs with which we speak in a certain way in silence, when wise caution forbids us to speak. For a signal to the elect, you place your left hand over your heart, then the right arm is elevated with the index finger pointing to the sky, and if [another] puts his left hand on his heart, so you extend your right arm in the prescribed manner.

9. For a signal of being baptized [*consolati*], you put three fingers apart on the forehead (your thumb and little finger must hit together). The other will grasp your hair with the index finger and the middle one. Then you rub with the index finger of the left hand the index finger of the right hand on the last limb, whereupon the other rubs the eyelids with three fingers of your right, as if you were anointing.

10. For a sign of invitation to the chapter, one whispers in the other's ear: "Night!" and if they cannot approach one another without arousing suspicion, one makes the sign of the night, then the other will answer to the first by the sign of either the elect or the baptized [*consolati*]. But the sign of the night is that you put your hand on the cheek.

11. For a sign of danger, either in battle or on the sea, extend hands and arms, crying: "Yah-Allah!" Wherever you may see this sign, and hear the call, hurry and bring as much help as you can to the caller.

12. For a sign of the Undershirt of the elect, extend all the fingers of one hand, and draw them together on the breast, as one that gathers wool. For a sign of the Belt, bring a finger around [another] finger and take the fingers of both hands from both sides as one who puts on his belt. For a sign of Baphomet, touch the back of the head with the right hand and rub the chin with the fingers of the left.

13. For a sign of the secret statutes, retract the fingers of both hand, alternately overlapping each other, one and two times apart, and

spread out the hand, as if from the chest, unfolds like something wrapped up. As a sign of the secret sciences, close your eyes and place your finger to your chest.

14. For a sign of resident brethren worthy of election, place the right forefinger on the forehead, and that of the left on the ear; as a sign of an unworthy, take the right index finger in the mouth and close your eyes. As a sign of resident brothers worthy of the baptism of fire [*consolamentum*], put the three middle fingers of the right hand together on the forehead; for a sign of an unworthy, put the same sign under the shirt or coat.

15. To denote that a monk, abbot, bishop, clergyman, or master of the sciences is worthy, draw the right hand from the right side down to the left and again from left to right. As a sign of rejection, put the right hand on the neck.

16. For a sign of the worthiness of a layman, take hold of the chin with the right hand, for sign of rejection, bring the little finger to the lips. For a sign of a master mason, place fist above fist in turns. For a sign of the great arts, strike with the fist upon the fist, because this signifies metal.

17. For a sign of good (because you will speak good), place your thumb on one cheek and the other fingers on the other and let them gently collapse under the chin. For a sign of evil, put the fingers spread on the face in the shape of the claw of a bird lacerating something. For a sign of a thing to be done immediately, place the hand evenly against the breast, so that the inner side of the hand is turned downwards, and thus move it more downwards from the breast.

18. For the sign of affirmation, raise the hand moderately and move it without turning it so that the surface is turned outwards and downwards. To denote negation, place the tip of the middle finger under the thumb and let it jump back.

Here ends the list of secret signs compiled by Master Brother Roncelinus and copied by me, Brother Robert of Samford. In the fortieth year of the light after the thousandth two hundredth Prid. Id. Augusti.

Postscript

Unfortunately, the highly-accomplished author of this paper has not been granted the experience of seeing this document reach the end of its printing. A stroke that struck him in the early hours of March 21, at the site of his official business, quickly and unexpectedly removed him from earthly existence. His hopelessly afflicted beloved son, under the gravest of sorrows until the last moment of his life, also soon followed him to death. Dr. Merzdorf, who was born on 25 August 1812 in Leipzig and reached the library of Oldenburg in his 29th year, made himself well-acclaimed through his numerous literary works, especially in the field of Masonic literature, so that, beside the already formerly passed away Dr. Kloss in Frankfurt a. M., he could be rightly called the most zealous and knowledgeable researcher of this field in modern times. Yet he was distinguished not only by his writings, but also by the important Masonic collections which he brought to light, attesting to his comprehensive and not insignificant activities. Apart from two collections of coins–one of which had been passed to Pythagoras' Lodge in New York, the other to the owner of what is presently the largest masonic catalogue, Herr von Bärenstein–he had a great number of valuable handwritten pieces, such as the complete works of Starck's clerical system, Hund's legitimacy dossier, the complete rituals of the Illuminati in a certified copy, etc., and a collection of masonry seals from 1900, mostly excellent specimens, acquired after his death by the highest Masonic body in Berlin, and thus preserved in the German homeland. Of course, his continuous correspondence with the members of the most varied systems was very widespread, and thus this whole relationship [between them] was also the reason, as he writes on page 24, that he was able to make *The Secret Statutes of the Templars*, which had been accessible in the archives of the great lodge in Hamburg. I shall add here to Findel's history of Freemasonry by adding here that he Russian State Counselor Böber, mentioned there, was, from 1811 to 1814, the Grandmaster of the Directorial "Vladimir zur Ordnung" (Swedish System) in St. Petersburg, which came into being in the autumn of 1808. Prince Muskin Pushkin was the successor of this position, which was dissolved after about 3 years, because on 12 August, 1822, the closing of all Masonic lodges in Russia took place.

On a note made by me, in reply to a letter from that immortal day of March 13 [the anniversary of the date on which many Cathars besieged on Montsegur received the *consolamentum* rite before being martyred three days later in the Albigensian Crusade]: "If the Templar's secret statutes are located in a corner of the Stockholm or Copenhagen archives (which I doubt after all my investigations so far), and are found to be in any way connected with the Swedish system, then you will also [see the connection]." Unfortunately, such an investigation has not been able to take place on its own, and it must be expected that the publication of the present writing may be the cause of inquiries and requests for publications from there.

I have to add that Dr. Merzdorf expressly wanted the "Secret Statutes" to be published as an addition to *The History of the Order of the Templars* of the top minister Dr. Ferdinand Wilcke, which was published in its second edition in two volumes in 1860, along with a report on Merzdorf's relationship with the Freemasons and the new Paris Templars.

Halle, [Germany], July 1877.
Dr. Gustav Schwetschke.

Tombstones located in the former chieftain house of the Templar Province of Portugal in Tomar
Photo:tomarterratemplariafotos.blogspot.fr/2011/07/estelas-funerarias-medievais.html"

From Article 30: *"The deceased brothers are to be buried with their red belt, and in their exequies the Mass of the Holy Spirit is to be administered in a red robe, but on the tombstone shall be the Pentalpha, the oldest sign of salvation."*

www.ingramcontent.com/pod-product-compliance
Lightning Source LLC
Chambersburg PA
CBHW070410200726
48294CB00003B/1152
* 9 7 8 1 9 6 2 3 1 2 0 8 0 *